D1491046

Mark May's
TALES FROM THE WASHINGTON REDSKINS

MARK MAY
WITH DAN O'BRIEN

www.SportsPublishingLLC.com

ISBN: 1-59670-082-3

Publishers: Peter L. Bannon and Joseph J. Bannon Sr.
Senior managing editor: Susan M. Moyer
Acquisitions editor: Scott Musgrave
Developmental editor: Travis W. Moran
Art director: K. Jeffrey Higgerson
Dust jacket design: Heidi Norsen
Interior layout: Kathryn R. Holleman
Imaging: Kathryn Holleman, Heidi Norsen, and Dustin Hubbart
Photo editor: Erin Linden-Levy
Media and promotions managers: Nick Obradovich (regional),
    Randy Fouts (national), Maurey Williamson (print)

Printed in the United States of America

Sports Publishing L.L.C.
804 North Neil Street
Champaign, IL 61820

Phone: 1-877-424-2665
Fax: 217-363-2073
www.SportsPublishingLLC.com

This book is dedicated to the true Washington Redskin fans who were at RFK Stadium through the good days, the bad days, the cold days, the wet days, and the snowy days, and still believed their Redskins could get the job done.

CONTENTS

INTRODUCTION

I doubt anything could have fully prepared me for my first ten seasons in the National Football League—all with the Washington Redskins. Oh, I was probably as well-equipped as possible. I had just finished four years at the University of Pittsburgh, surrounded by great coaches and great players. In fact, two of my Pitt teammates—Hugh Green and Randy McMillan—would join me as first-round selections in the 1981 NFL draft.

I had played in major bowl games for teams that challenged for the national championship—and received national media exposure, including the 1980 Outland Trophy as the nation's top interior lineman.

Yet, life on a college campus—even an urban campus like Pitt—is isolated somewhat from the "real world." In many ways, I was still the small-town kid from upstate New York—granted, at six foot six and 285 pounds, I was a very big kid, but a kid nonetheless.

I was suddenly thrust into a world I could hardly imagine while growing up in Oneonta, New York. There is no other city in the world like Washington, D.C. Everyone you see is in office, running for office, or lobbying someone in office. The small-town boy soon found himself meeting high-powered lobbyists, congressmen, senators and, yes, even the president and first lady of the United States.

Yes, our nation's capital is like no other city. If I can add to that, Washington Redskins fans are like no others in the National Football League. The people of the Washington metropolitan area love their Redskins, even when times are tough. Once we hit our stride, the tough times for Redskin rooters were rare. Despite playing in one of the NFL's toughest divisions, we won five division titles, made three trips to the Super Bowl, and walked away with the Lombardi Trophy in Super Bowls XVII and XXII.

We were a team in the true sense of the word. We liked playing together. We liked hanging around together. We had

Charlie Casserly (left), a Redskins scout, assistant general manager, and general manager was one of the people most responsible for me becoming a Washington Redskin. This was the day the Redskins retired my jersey.

certain groups who were known for their own thing and had their fan clubs and followers—"The Hogs," "The Fun Bunch," "The Smurfs," and "The Wrecking Crew." They were never a source of resentment or jealousy, at least as far as I could tell. Eventually, those groups combined. We hung together and shared a special camaraderie.

When I started broadcasting games with TNT or CBS, I'd visit practices. Particularly early in a season, I could sense if a team was unified by one simple observation: After practice, did everybody sprint to their cars to get away as quickly as possible? Or did they hang around a while, maybe lift weights together, or go have a cold one?

Even though some teams looked better or worse on paper, I could tell—usually about 80 percent of the time—which teams would be successful. I learned that from the Washington Redskins.

There's a great scene in the movie *Hoosiers* (which gets a number of votes as the top sports film of all time). The teacher, played by Barbara Hershey, complains to the basketball coach that basketball players in Indiana are treated like gods.

The coach, played by Gene Hackman, replies, "Most people would give their life to be treated like a god, if even for a few minutes."

As members of the Washington Redskins, we were treated like gods often—for an entire decade. With that kind of adulation comes, or should come, a greater level of responsibility. I realize all of us didn't live up to that all of the time. I know I didn't. I made my mistakes, but my experiences with the Redskins allowed me to grow as a player and as a person. I'd like to think I hit the mark most of the time.

Chapter One

GETTING STARTED

I'm sure most Redskin fans think my affiliation with the Washington Redskins began with the 1981 draft. No, it goes back much further than that—back to the spring of 1978 when I was a mere freshman at the University of Pittsburgh. Tom Brzoza, our All-America center, was going through some drills for Redskins scouts at Pitt Stadium.

I was working out, getting ready to start my sophomore season for the Panthers. I had started several games and played in just about all of them as a freshman.

Of course, one of the standard drills for any scouting workout is the 40-yard dash. One of the scouts had Tom off to the side, timing him in the 40.

I was jogging on the track that circled the football field. The scout asked me if I'd like to participate, just to give Tom Brzoza someone to run against. Mind you, Tom Brzoza was a senior All-America center, weighing about 260 pounds. I was a freshman, weighing about 290 pounds.

I ran against Tom Brzoza, and I beat him the first time. We ran a second 40 with the same result.

That was really the beginning of my affiliation with the Washington Redskins. The man with the stopwatch that day was Charlie Casserly, who would later become assistant to Redskins general manager Bobby Beathard. Charlie succeeded Bobby Beathard as Redskins general manager. He is currently the general manager of the Houston Texans.

Charlie told me to work hard, stay in school, and continue to play football the best I could. If I was lucky and stayed healthy, I might be drafted by the Washington Redskins. Three years later, it came to fruition.

Charlie's "stay in school" advice might seem superfluous to a sophomore-to-be, particularly in light of the recent court case involving Maurice Clarett and his attempt to gain early entry into the National Football League. The NFL wasn't a viable alternative then, either, but pro football wasn't entirely out of the question.

After my freshman season at the University of Pittsburgh, an agent for the Montreal Allouettes of the Canadian Football League contacted my teammate Hugh Green and me. I received a six-figure offer from Montreal, which was a hell of a lot of money at the time. Charlie's words of wisdom weren't totally out of the blue. Fortunately, I heeded his advice and stayed in school. Leaving for the CFL would have been an enormous mistake at that point in my life.

Montreal approached me again after my senior season. I never had any serious intentions of signing with the CFL, but the interest from the CFL paid big dividends in negotiations with the Redskins. It's better to be a Hog than a hoser, eh?

◆　◆　◆

April 28, 1981—I wish I could remember all the important dates in my life as readily as that one comes to mind. That was the first day of the 1981 NFL draft and my first "official" association with the Redskins.

The Redskins picked me all right, just as Charlie Casserly said they might three years earlier. It didn't go entirely as planned, though.

The Redskins called me early on draft day. They had the ninth and 20th picks in the first round. I found out later the Redskins had me rated as the ninth best player overall in the draft, so the numbers worked out perfectly. Washington general manager Bobby Beathard told me, "If you're available, we're going to select you."

So I settled in, ready to be selected ninth by the Washington Redskins. Instead the Redskins traded their initial first-round pick to the Los Angeles Rams for a third-round pick and two fifth-round choices in the 1981 draft as well as the Rams' second pick the following season.

Those moves eventually worked out pretty well for the Redskins. At the time, though, I was thinking, "What the hell is going on? Am I going to be picked or not?"

The Redskins still wanted me and took a gamble that I'd still be around for the 20th pick. Apparently they heard that the two teams expecting to take offensive linemen ahead of them—the Bears and the Patriots—had other picks in mind. Sure enough, Chicago took USC's Keith Van Horne with the 11th pick, and the Patriots selected Stanford's Brian Holloway with the 19th selection.

Bobby kept his promise. When the Redskins got their chance—with the 20th pick—I was their man. I didn't realize it at the time, but that was a small landmark in the career of the Redskins' new head coach. I was Joe Gibbs's first ever draft pick.

◆ ◆ ◆

I don't know how the experts today rate the 1981 NFL draft, but I'm proud to have been a first-rounder with that group. Lawrence Taylor and Ronnie Lott were also first-round selections that year. Mike Singletary and Howie Long were drafted in the second round. All four are in the Pro Football Hall of Fame.

Just before the 2005 NFL draft, I did read one article that rated the best draft years by individual teams. The Washington Redskins' 1981 draft placed sixth in that particular rating. I realize I'm a little biased, but I think that's a bit low for us. I can't make a huge fuss over their No. 1 selection—1974 Steelers—a draft class that included Hall of Famers Jack Lambert, Lynn Swann, John Stallworth, and Mike Webster.

I still think we could give them a run for their money, especially if you look at the Redskins' overall acquisitions that year, not just those selected in the draft.

On Draft Day 1981, the Redskins traded their No. 2 pick to Baltimore for veteran running back Joe Washington. Barry Switzer said Washington was his greatest player ever at Oklahoma. Joe probably weighed about 175 pounds in full pads. If he had any size, he might have been declared illegal. Pro football fans probably best remember Joe with the Colts and the one-man show he performed on *Monday Night Football* against the Patriots in 1978. But Joe had some great years with us, too, before injuries slowed him down. Joe used to describe his running style as "smoke through a keyhole."

In the third round, we picked up my Pitt teammate, Russ Grimm. Originally slated to be a center, Russ went to four consecutive Pro Bowls at offensive guard and is a 2005 finalist for the NFL Hall of Fame. Russ, like his old Pitt teammate, was a charter member of The Hogs—the Redskins' offensive line.

In the fifth round, we got Dexter Manley, one of the most awesome physical talents I've ever seen on a football field. Dexter was a perennial All-Pro until his well-documented personal problems derailed his career.

Charlie Brown, an unheralded wide receiver from South Carolina State, was the team's eighth-round pick. Charlie also became a Pro Bowler.

Darryl Grant joined us in the ninth round. Darryl was an offensive guard at Rice but developed into a long-time starter at defensive tackle. This is a personal favorite pick of mine since Darryl was my roommate on the road and at training camp. He remains a good friend.

Our 12th-round pick was Clint Didier from Portland State. Clint was kind of a hybrid tight end-wide receiver, probably the first true H-Back in the NFL.

Our free agent acquisitions included Joe Jacoby and Mel Kaufman. Big "Jake" was another original Hog and regular Pro Bowl participant. Mel played for a NCAA Division II championship team at Cal-Poly San Luis Obispo and became a regular for us, starting at linebacker in three Super Bowls.

Now, that's one hell of a class.

◆ ◆ ◆

Shortly after drafting me, the Redskins contacted me about flying into Washington for a press conference. They asked if I was up for it. Are you kidding me? I was pumped; I was psyched.

Up for it? I couldn't wait to get on the plane.

As I was preparing to fly from Pittsburgh National to Washington Dulles airport, I started to think silly things like, "I'll bet Senator So-and-So used this same gate," or "I'll be walking the same terminal as a supreme court justice." Hey, I told you there still was some of the small-town kid left.

But when I stepped off that plane at Dulles, I was wide-eyed for a different reason. To this day, that was the worst flight I've ever taken. A monstrous thunderstorm hit us about midway through the flight—lightning everywhere. There was incredible

Settling into training was like moving back into an old apartment. At the time this photo was taken, those pants were "stylish"—even off the golf course.

turbulence. We lost altitude. I thought the plane was going down.

Now, I'm sure you've heard stories about people who kiss the ground after such an experience. Usually, that's an exaggeration, but I can honestly say I came real close to doing just that. Once we landed at Dulles, once I reached the terminal gate, I kissed the side of the wall and said, "Thank God I made it; I'm here at last." I decided then that I would DRIVE back to Pittsburgh.

◆ ◆ ◆

As I pulled myself together, I noticed there was someone waiting to talk with me, someone I recognized right away—Sonny Jurgensen.

Sonny is an icon in Washington. For that matter, he's a legend throughout the National Football League. When you hear discussions about the greatest "pure passers" in football history, Sonny's name is almost sure to arise.

He was one of the game's early "gunslingers," a quarterback who helped usher in the more wide-open passing game we see today. In 1967, the Washington Redskins had the No. 1 (Charley Taylor), No. 2 (Jerry Smith), and No. 4 (Bobby Mitchell) receivers in the NFL—all at the receiving end of bullets.

I learned about those numbers later. My earliest recollections of Sonny Jurgensen—when I was old enough to really start following pro football—were the battles between Billy Kilmer and him for the Redskins' starting quarterback slot.

Here we are on April 28, 1981, a couple years before Sonny's induction into the Pro Football Hall of Fame. Sonny was working as a sportscaster for the local CBS television affiliate. He was there with a cameraman for my first TV interview as the Redskins' top draft pick (this was pre-9/11 security when you could go right up to the gate with a camera).

He asked me the basic questions: How does it feel to be a Washington Redskin? Are you excited to be here? What can you do to help the team?

Not exactly a mind-boggling interrogation, but I was trying to say all the right things while attempting to shake the memories of the "flight from hell."

Sonny concluded the interview and said, "Congratulations, and good luck."

I smiled, shook his hand, and replied, "Hey, thanks a lot. I really appreciate it, *Billy*."

If only that were the end of a shaky beginning in Washington.

◆ ◆ ◆

One of my first memories as a Redskin—as a member of the team—is the 1981 training camp. I had a rough camp. I held out a couple weeks before reporting, and I had lost some muscle mass. The 285-pound tackle they drafted showed up at 264 pounds that year.

I got into a fistfight every day with Fred Cook, a defensive lineman they brought over from the Baltimore Colts. I think the coaches set it up to challenge me. Every day in the one-on-one drills, they'd call out, "May! Cook!"

We'd start our drill, and "Bam-Bam-Bam," a fight would break out—every day, twice a day, for nearly my entire training camp. Finally, near the end of training camp, the fights with Cook decreased. I was tested, not only by Fred Cook and the coaches, but also by other players. I got into fistfights with Rich Milot, Neal Olkewicz, and a few others.

Veterans have a way of "introducing" rookies to the NFL. You might as well get your initiation in training camp with your teammates, because the opposition sure isn't going to give you an easy ride. Still, it seemed as if I were getting into more than my fair share of altercations.

Most of it was probably my fault. I guess I was the kind of guy who could've had a chip on my shoulder, but that's how my career started.

ROOKIE HAZING NIGHT

The hazing of rookies at training camp has subsided around the NFL in recent years. When I played, it was "no holds barred."

During training camp, the veterans would flood us out of our dormitory rooms, "smoke" us out of our rooms with fire extinguishers, force us to strip and run around, and hit us with belts. It was awful.

Darryl Grant was my roommate in rookie training camp (as he would be throughout my Redskin career). We knew the worst night would be the last night at camp. There was a construction site near the dorm, so I convinced Darryl that we should build a little wall inside our room.

We wedged some 2x4s and 4x8s against our door so the vets couldn't enter. We stuffed wet towels under our door so they couldn't get water into the room or use the fire extinguishers. We settled in for a night of peaceful bliss.

One of the assistant coaches, Torgy Torgeson—probably prompted by the veterans—knocked on our door later, claiming he was making a "bed check." Torgy tried to persuade us to open the door to verify we were in our room—as if our voices through the door weren't proof. Torgy even threatened to fine us if we didn't open up. Sorry, Torgy. … Nothing doing.

Although that was the last night in camp, we had one more day of practice before we all high-tailed it out of Carlisle. Darryl and I thought for sure we would get double trouble for our efforts. The vets ran us around the practice field, knocked us around, stripped us down to our jockstraps, and dumped cold water on us in the middle of the practice field.

But it was minor compared to what they did to the others. We dodged that bullet.

◆ ◆ ◆

That first year was a disaster for me personally and nearly for the team—at least initially. We started 0-5. In my first regular-season game with the Washington Redskins, I went in at left tackle—a position I had never played (I was a right tackle at Pitt). It was our home opener against the Dallas Cowboys. I had to line up across two of the best defensive linemen in pro football: Harvey Martin and Randy White.

So here's Mark May, a rookie at left tackle, and Russ Grimm, a rookie at left guard, against the All-Pro right side of the Dallas defensive line. And we weren't the only newcomers. We used about a dozen guys who had never played before in the NFL and four new starters on the offensive line.

Surprisingly, it wasn't that bad. We shut out Martin and White in the first half—no sacks, no hurries—and we were only seven points behind the Cowboys at halftime, 14-7. Russ and I started talking a little "smack," which probably wasn't the smartest move. The Cowboys got a little more revved up in the second half, got a couple sacks, and won the game, 26-10.

We didn't win our first game until we played the Bears in Chicago. In that game I ended up fracturing my nose in about 30 places. That was just one of the injuries that led to my removal as a starter.

I was benched about three-quarters through my rookie season. I had a sprained knee, a hip pointer, and a broken nose. I can't argue with the results, though. My replacement, Joe Jacoby, quickly developed into one of the best left tackles in the game.

That year was a difficult year. During that winless start, we heard much criticism and questions as to whether the new coach, Joe Gibbs, or the veteran quarterback, Joe Theismann, were the right guys to lead us. We rallied and ended up 8-8 for the year, missing the playoffs by only one game. That was respectable and quieted some of the critics, but it was still a tough year for yours truly.

Chapter Two

THE FRONT OFFICE AND ADMINISTRATION

THE OWNER

One of the great privileges I enjoyed during my career with the Redskins was playing for owner Jack Kent Cooke. For some reason, I felt he always liked me, and I always got along with Mr. Cooke. He was good to me and so was the Cooke family. I had the greatest respect for him and his son, John. Mr. Cooke always called his son, "Johnny Cakes." Some of the players joked about that, but I never did.

Jack Kent Cooke brought me to the Redskins at the beginning of my career and brought me back so I could retire as a Redskin. To retire a Redskin after spending so many great seasons in Washington was special in my career.

As much as I admired and respected him, I probably didn't know as much about Mr. Cooke as I should have, at least not when I played for him. A few years after I retired from football, I was working for Turner Sports. The producers asked if I could set up an interview with Mr. Cooke. I wasn't sure if he'd consent. Mr. Cooke didn't grant many interviews. Occasionally, he'd agree to a local interview but not many on the national level. Fortunately he consented to my request.

Sure I knew Jack Kent Cooke was a wealthy and powerful man, but through my research and during the course of the interview, I discovered a number of amazing things he had accomplished.

A native Canadian, the former encyclopedia salesman was a self-made billionaire, amassing his fortune in newspapers, television, and sports—just to name a few of his ventures.

In addition to owning the Washington Redskins, he once owned the Los Angeles Lakers and the Los Angeles Kings. He built the L.A. forum and owned the Chrysler Building in New York City. He essentially created pay-per-view for mega sporting events when he financed the first Ali-Frazier fight.

He also entered the *Guinness Book of World Records* with the divorce settlement of his first marriage—a then-record $41 million. But you can look up those stories. I have a few personal tales.

◆   ◆   ◆

When I was with the Redskins, we had little extra incentives for performances, a little slush fund from people in the Redskin "community" who liked to donate to the program. The Hogs had one. For instance, if we rushed the ball for 150 or 175 yards, we'd get "X" amount donated to the kitty. Or if we gave up no sacks, a certain amount went into the collection.

In a good season, we'd have several thousand dollars in our fund by season's end. We rented limousines and made reservations at one of the finest dining establishments in the Washington metropolitan area. We dressed up in tuxedos, top hats, and canes. Of course, as Hogs, we had to deviate slightly from this formal attire. We all wore tennis shoes with the tuxes.

We'd do it one time with our wives or girlfriends and then again with just the fellow Hogs. On one of our stag outings, we went to The Palm, a tremendous establishment in Washington, a preferred dining spot for many of the area's powerbrokers. In fact, The Palm boasts on its website: If you can't find your representative on Capitol Hill, you better check The Palm. Larry King and Tim Russert are known regulars at The Palm, as was Jack Kent Cooke in his day.

We had a little private room, and we were having a great time—eating, drinking, and partying. Well, word got out that The Hogs were in the house, and a couple of Redskin fans sent us a bottle of champagne. No, it was a couple bottles of champagne.

I couldn't have played for a better owner, "The Squire," Mr. Jack Kent Cooke (seated, second from the left), shown here at one of our functions at Redskin Park. Seated next to Mr. Cooke (in the wide-brimmed hat) is his fourth wife, Marlene—the "Bolivian Bombshell"—in one of her more sedate moments.

Naturally, after the first two bottles we decided some additional libation was necessary to wash down the 10-pound lobsters and four-pound steaks. We ordered a few more bottles of the bubbly. We had about $7,000 in our kitty, which normally was enough—even for a Hog feast. This time, though, our bill was close to $8,500.

George Starke, our elder statesman, the Head Hog, was unruffled by the slight deficiency.

"Don't worry about it," George said. "Mr. Cooke has a tab here. We'll put it on his bill."

Huge—HUUUUGE—mistake!

I'm told pigs are very intelligent animals. Well, these Hogs had their heads in the trough on this one. We should have remembered the old adage: Pigs get fed; Hogs get slaughtered.

The next day we had an easy schedule to tap: a little stretching and watch films. Just as the film session gets ready to start, Joe Gibbs comes over, grabs George Starke, and hauls him into his office.

"I've been on the phone with Mr. Cooke the last 40 minutes," he told George. "He wanted to fire me. He wanted to fire everybody involved. I've been able to save your job. But Mr. Cooke wants his money, and he wants it NOW. Not tomorrow, not later this afternoon—NOW!"

George came back and relayed the message: "Guys, we have to come up with $1,500 ASAP."

You're probably thinking, "What's $1,500 to a billionaire?"

That's not the point. We messed with *his* money. "Now" was not a negotiable term. We had less than 30 minutes, not enough time to get to the bank and back.

So we ended up scurrying around the locker room and Redskin Park, borrowing five dollars here, ten dollars there with an occasional jackpot: "Hey, this guy's got $200."

We had to borrow money from defensive players who loved watching us beg.

Finally we scraped enough together. We saved everyone's job and learned a very valuable lesson: Don't mess with The Squire's money.

◆ ◆ ◆

For some reason Mr. Cooke took to calling me "George" when he saw me, somehow confusing me with George Starke. I'll admit there's a slight resemblance, but George is much older, and I'm much better looking (hey, let George refute it in *his* book).

Actually, Mr. Cooke wasn't the only one who confused us. Even to this day, people will call him "Mark" or me "George." When we played together with the Redskins, Mr. Starke would occasionally take it to another step.

Most of the time, George and I both got some big laughs over it, but occasionally the mistaken identity became an irritant. One day I was in the bathroom at Redskin Park. It had not been a particularly good day for me, and Mr. Cooke walked in. We were the only two in the bathroom at that time. I wasn't in a very hospitable mood, but I turned to him and said, "Hello, Mr. Cooke, how are you today?"

"I'm just fabulous, *George*," he replied. "And how are you?"

Normally, I'd laugh off the George reference, but every now and then, it would get under my skin a bit. I felt myself thinking, "Look, you blind old codger. I'm not George. I'm Mark. I'm Mark May. Just because we're both tall, black, and wear mustaches, we're not the same person. We're not all the same."

A moment of panic nearly overwhelmed me as I thought, "Oh, my God. Did I say that *out loud?*"

I looked at Mr. Cooke's smiling face and said, "Just fine, Mr. Cooke, just fine."

◆ ◆ ◆

We always addressed Jack Kent Cooke as "Mr. Cooke," never "Jack" and certainly not "The Squire." We really didn't mean any disrespect by that nickname, but I don't think Mr. Cooke would have appreciated the humor.

Everyone in the Redskin organization received "suggestions" on what to do and say in Mr. Cooke's presence. Club management, however, neglected our etiquette lessons for an audience with the president of the United States. When we flew back to Washington after winning our first Super Bowl, the president and first lady—Ronald and Nancy Reagan—were at the airport to greet our plane. There was a little receiving line for all of us right on the tarmac.

I became increasingly nervous as I stood in the line to meet the Reagans. "What do I do? What do I say? How do I act?" Suddenly, I got the bright idea: "Hey, this is American *royalty*, right?"

That's my wife, Kathy, and I flanking the president and first lady, George and Barbara Bush. NFL players in other cities might be invited to functions with the mayor. In Washington, we aim a little higher.

When my turn came, I gave the president a firm handshake and politely responded, "Thank you, Mr. President," to his warm congratulations. Then I grabbed Mrs. Reagan's, bowed ever so gallantly, and kissed it. You got it. I kissed the hand of the first lady of the United States.

As you might expect, Mrs. Reagan accepted the gesture with her usual grace. But she had to be thinking, "Who is this boob?"

Maybe that's a commentary on priorities in the NFL. We got instructions on how to act in front of the team owner. With the president and first lady, we were on our own.

◆ ◆ ◆

Mr. Cooke could be extremely generous, but it had to be on his terms. He knew how to squeeze a dollar. Mr. Cooke was known to throw big, lavish parties at his estate in the mountains of northern Virginia, where many of the high-society types lived. Mr. Cooke would order the finest linens and china from the swankiest stores in the area.

The day after the party, the billionaire would call them up and say, "Come and get it. It's not the highest quality. It's not good enough. And I want every nickel back."

And that's exactly what they did.

◆ ◆ ◆

I think Mr. Cooke was prouder of our first Super Bowl victory in the Rose Bowl than he was of any of his other achievements. Here's a man who had owned the Lakers and built the L.A. Forum. He had returned to *his* town, ready to strut *his* stuff with *his* Redskins.

I'll never forget Mr. Cooke's words when he accepted the Lombardi Trophy. You have to understand that there was a long-standing hatred between Mr. Cooke and NFL Commissioner Pete Rozelle. One of Jack Kent Cook's

"Can I keep it?" Mr. Cooke asked when NFL Commissioner Pete Rozelle presented him the Lombardi Trophy after we won Super Bowl XVII. That young guy with the cap on the far right is then-second-year head coach and future Hall of Famer Joe Gibbs.

daughters-in-law left Mr. Cooke's son and ended up marrying Rozelle. They hated each other, never talked.

When Rozelle handed the trophy to Mr. Cooke, he gave the usual speech: "Congratulations, Jack Kent Cooke, you are winners of Super Bowl XVII."

Mr. Cooke grabbed the trophy, looked Rozelle right in the eye, and belted out, "Is it mine, forever and ever. Can I keep it?"

◆ ◆ ◆

I was in the car business in the Washington metro area—a business I learned from my good friend Rick Hunt, who did business with Mr. Cooke. Rick could tell some great stories of Mr. Cooke's thrifty habits.

Mr. Cooke used to ride in an old limousine. It was probably 15 years old. He would run down something until he got every nickel, every penny out of anything. He didn't care. I guess when you're a billionaire you don't have to.

One day, Mr. Cooke decided he wanted tinted windows on his limo. He took the limo to Rick Hunt's dealership.

"No problem, Mr. Cooke," Rick said. "We'll take care of the whole thing for you."

"No, no . . . no, no, no," Mr. Cooke responded in his very distinctive, raspy voice. "I already went out and purchased the tint."

He had done just that. This mogul—owner of one of the most valuable pro sports franchises—had gone out and purchased tint at some five-and-dime store, those cheap rolls of tint that you roll out by hand. Mr. Cooke wanted Rick's employees to apply the tint while he observed the operation from inside the car.

This happened in late July, one of those days when it's about 95 degrees and scorching humidity, where you're just walking outside and sweat rolls from under your armpits and down the side of your cheeks.

Mr. Cooke and his driver sat in the car and watched the "rolling of the tint." Rick offered to take Mr. Cooke and his driver to lunch, more to give them a break from the heat than anything else.

"Oh, no, no, no, no," Mr. Cooke said. "We have lunch. We're just fine right here."

He opened the glove compartment and pulled out some cheese crackers, those square little crackers with the processed cheese in the middle. He sent the driver out for a bottle of water and a bottle of soda. The two proceeded to sit in the back of the limo—where it was probably 100 degrees—eating cheese and crackers while they watched the guys put the tint on the window.

The same man who put up $2.5 million each for Ali and Frazier in 1971 wouldn't spend an extra $30-50 for the dealer's tint—just the hourly wage to have the cheapo stuff applied.

◆ ◆ ◆

We always knew when Mr. Cooke was coming to practice—either at training camp or during the regular season—because a member of the public relations staff would put out two or three chairs. We knew then that "The Squire" was coming to practice. His guests were usually some type of celebrity or dignitary, a big name in the media or a political heavyweight. Leslie Stahl, Larry King, and Bernard Shaw were among the media stars who joined Mr. Cooke at our practice sessions. Aaron Latham, whose screenwriting credits include *Urban Cowboy, Perfect,* and *The Program,* was one of Mr. Cooke's regular guests. Kevin Costner even made an appearance, as did Arnold Schwarzenegger and Maria Shriver. Senator John Warner, a member of the Redskins' board, was another frequent celebrity visitor.

Our preseason training camp was located at Dickinson College—a Division III school in the Eastern Pennsylvania town of Carlisle. Dickinson has a wonderful small college campus. However, there wasn't much parking available because our fans came out in big numbers, even for training camp. Unless you arrived early, you had to walk about three or four blocks to get to the practice facility.

Once, when we were in the middle of two-a-day practices, I arrived tired and sore. I didn't see any chairs out by the practice field, so I figured I could park in Mr. Cooke's spot. I still asked—believe me, I asked. I was told he wasn't coming.

Lo and behold, Mr. Cooke decided to surprise everyone and come to Carlisle to watch practice. He drove up to the facility, saw a car in his spot and immediately flagged down John Kanoza, who worked in the PR department.

Mr. Cooke: "John, whose car is that?"

John: "I don't know, Mr. Cooke."

Well, John did know, but he wasn't about to let on.

Mr. Cooke: "I want the bloody culprit found. I want his name, I want that vehicle tagged, I want it towed, and I want that bloody person off my football team today."

John hunted me down and said, "May Day, I need your keys pronto. I have to move your car. Mr. Cooke's here, and he wants your butt kicked off the team."

John went back to move my car, hoping he could do so without Mr. Cooke noticing—no such luck.

Mr. Cooke: "Now Kanoza, whose car is that?"

John: "Uh, Mr. Cooke, that's Mark May's car."

John waited for the eruption. Fortunately, Mr. Cooke had his priorities straight.

Mr. Cooke: "Oh no, no, no. We need him. Just tell him to move his car expeditiously."

John moved the car posthaste—another catastrophe averted.

◆   ◆   ◆

At the end of mini-camps, we always had a little barbecue. Attending this particular function was Mr. Cooke's fourth wife, Marlene, and her two little kids. Marlene was a wild one, sometimes referred to as the Bolivian Bombshell. She spent some time in prison, and she once was arrested for driving around Georgetown with a boyfriend on the hood of her Jaguar.

Bobby Beathard started throwing a football back and forth to one of the kids. A bunch of the players started watching, figuring this could be a recipe for disaster. Sure enough, Bobby threw the ball back to the kid, and he whiffed it.

Whack! It smacked him right in the side of the head.

The kid started screaming and ran to his mother. Bobby had no idea how she would react or what she might tell Mr. Cooke. He turned immediately and started pointing his finger at Charlie Casserly, his assistant. Charlie was standing nearby, but he had nothing to do with it.

Where there's smoke, there are Hogs—at least for a barbecue at the May estate.

Nobody saw it but us. We sat on the back of somebody's truck and laughed like hell. There was one of the most respected general managers in the NFL pointing his finger after an innocent accident with a little kid.

Fortunately, Bobby survived that minor fiasco.

◆   ◆   ◆

Jack Kent Cooke always did things in a big way—even when he passed away. His funeral was an extraordinary event, certainly the biggest funeral I'll ever attend. The big names in Washington were there, as was a Who's Who of Hollywood.

Most of my old teammates were there, including Joe Jacoby. We started talking with Tony Kornheiser, reminiscing and trading Jack Kent Cooke stories. It's amazing, though, how conversations will drift at a funeral—probably to break the tension. Joe and I were both in the car business at the time, so the conversation shifted to cars.

Tony was chomping at the bit to get into this one. He started gushing over his new car. I believe it was an Allante, the new small Cadillac that came out in the mid-'90s. Whatever the make or model, Joe and I were ready. We knew Tony was in love with the car because he used to talk about it on his radio show in Washington. We knew we could bust his chops, although we didn't quite plan for it to happen at a memorial service.

We told Tony his new car was nothing but a Malibu with a fancy grill and leather seats. You would have thought we had just dissed his wife or mother. He was livid and told us we—the car dealers—didn't know what we were talking about and that we were just envious. Of course, the madder he got, the more we busted on him.

"Tony," we said. "We'll take a car from one of our lots, put a new grill on it, and you call it anything you want. We'll be happy to charge you five times what it was worth."

I love you, Tony—the only guy I know who was born with a Tootsie Roll wrapped around his head.

◆   ◆   ◆

When Jack Kent Cooke owned the Redskins, you got whatever you needed to win. I truly believe he tried to do the right thing by us. He could be mean and nasty to everyone else, but he was always true to form with his beloved Redskins.

◆   ◆   ◆

I was able to fool Bobby in one aspect of my contract negotiations. For years, Bobby thought it was my agent, Ralph Cindrich, who was the bad guy, holding out and needling Bobby for that extra little incentive or bonus.

It was me the whole time. I always orchestrated it with Ralph on what I wanted, what I was and wasn't going to do. Ralph accepted the bad-guy role. It was never "Mark wants this or Mark wants that." It was "WE gotta have this, WE gotta have that."

Bobby used to get so ticked off at Ralph. He'd come up to me and say, "May Day, I love the way you play, and it's great to have you around. But that SOB Cindrich is tough to deal with."

Bobby, if you only knew.

♦　♦　♦

In 1985, when I threatened to go to the USFL, I got some unexpected negotiating help. I never had any serious intentions about signing with Donald Trump's team. Sure, I paid a visit to the New Jersey Generals and met with Trump and Herschel Walker. I never wanted to leave the Redskins; it was just a ruse.

Once I heard that Jack Kent Cooke told Bobby Beathard, "We will not lose Mark May," I knew I had them by the onions. I got the Redskins to kick up another $100,000, which I'm sure Bobby blamed on Ralph.

As long as we're on the subject of Ralph Cindrich, please allow me to make a quick plug; fully realizing it's not popular to say nice things about agents and lawyers. Believe me, I don't make a habit of it. I'm one of those guys who reaches for the remote when the Oscar winners start thanking their agents. But Ralph Cindrich was my first and only agent and will always be my legal representation as far as sports and entertainment are concerned.

Of much greater value, though, is the friendship I have with Ralph and his family. From day one, we've had a bond. Ralph, his wife, Mary, son Michael, and daughter Christina are among my most cherished friends.

THE GENERAL MANAGER

While playing for the Redskins, I developed a closeness to a number of people in the front office—people like Bobby Beathard, Charlie Casserly, Billy Devaney, and Dickie Daniels. They were great guys and probably the best in the business at what they did.

Bobby Beathard should join Joe Gibbs in the Hall of Fame. I can't think of anybody in football who was better at evaluating talent or fitting together the right pieces of the puzzle.

Bobby had a hand in taking four teams to Super Bowls. He was a scout for the Kansas City Chiefs in the 1960s when the Chiefs went to the first Super Bowl. He was player personnel director at Miami when the Dolphins went to three straight Super Bowls. Bobby was the Redskins' general manager for

Longtime GM Bobby Beathard (far right) was one of the shrewdest in league history when it came to judging talent. On the left is Marty Hurney, a former Washington sportswriter who became a Beathard protégé. Marty is now general manager of the Carolina Panthers.

three Super Bowl appearances and two Super Bowl championships. He was general manager in San Diego for the Chargers' only Super Bowl appearance.

If you visited one of our practices at Redskin Park and didn't know Bobby Beathard, he's about the last guy you'd figure for the team's general manager. You'd swear he was just some fan who wandered in from a morning jog.

Bobby is an avid runner and surfer. I understand he even had a clause in his NFL contract that allowed him a day off in April for the Boston Marathon. His wardrobe was ultra-casual—a T-shirt and running shorts were his standard attire. We used to joke that he didn't own more than one pair of long pants or a suit. I remember seeing Bobby in a sport coat once in ten years.

But never let the casual attire or the blond bangs fool you. Bobby Beathard was one of the shrewdest men in the game.

THE COACH

Joe Gibbs is probably the most composed person I've ever been around, particularly in pressure situations. I think everybody is familiar with Joe Gibbs's religious convictions. I'm sure that plays a part in his normally calm demeanor.

However, everyone has his boiling point. When Joe finally reaches his, it is a double boiler. It didn't happen often. I saw him blow only a handful of times in ten years.

The first time I saw Joe really lose it was at training camp in 1983. We had this rookie wide receiver named Carl Powell, a third-round pick from Jackson State. He was a gamble since he played in a run-oriented offense in college and didn't catch many passes. But he had great physical tools—good size, great speed. He also had a reputation for not liking to run pass routes across the middle of the field.

Carl Powell did not have what it takes to be an NFL receiver. He had the big eyes, the deer-in-headlights look. He didn't have any guts; everybody learned that in a hurry. He was easily intimidated by everyone.

One day at camp we were in the middle of an early passing drill. It was a very simple drill: the receiver goes out, catches the ball, and concentrates.

Simple.

Well, Powell cut over the middle, heard footsteps, and just let the ball hit the ground.

Gibbs went berserk. He started screaming at the top of his lungs, "GO GET THE BALL! YOU GET THE BALL! YOU GO GET THE BALL RIGHT NOW!"

The kid just froze. He did not move. He didn't look at the ball, didn't look at Gibbs. He just stood there—immobile—for about ten seconds while Gibbs railed on him.

That was pretty much the end of Carl Powell with the Washington Redskins.

◆ ◆ ◆

Anybody who has followed the Redskins over the last 20 years would probably pick Darrell Green as the least likely candidate to cause Joe Gibbs to snap. Darrell was one of the all-around cornerbacks of all time—great on coverage and run support. He was one of the fastest men in the league, a great kick returner, tough as nails, a hard worker, a first-class citizen off the field, and extremely loyal. Darrell played 20 seasons in the NFL, all with the Washington Redskins. In short, everything you could possibly want in a football player.

So what did Darrell do to light Bunsy's fuse? It was during the strike of 1987. We had a strike meeting, and Darrell started saying we should cross the line and come back. Then he started voicing his opinion on what the coaches should do. That's when Bunsy flipped.

"WHAT ARE YOU TALKING ABOUT?" Bunsy yelled. "WHO ARE YOU TO TELL US WHAT TO DO? YOU NEED TO GET YOUR PRIORITIES STRAIGHT. WHICH SIDE OF THE LINE ARE YOU ON?"

The more he bellowed, the redder he turned and the more the vein in his neck popped out.

I don't want to paint the wrong picture about Joe Gibbs. As I wrote earlier, he was one of the best at staying calm in pressure situations. I guess it is because the outbursts happened so infrequently that they stand out so clearly in my mind.

◆ ◆ ◆

One thing about Joe Gibbs: no matter how mad he got, he never cussed. You'd never hear Joe Gibbs say something like, "Get your ass in gear."

With Joe it was always, "Move your buns" or "Run your buns off." So we started calling him "Buns" or "Bunsy."

After a particular meltdown at Philadelphia, R.C. Thielemann remarked, "I never thought a man could be that mad and say that many things without using one curse word."

We deserved a few choice words that day in Philly. We played like crap in the first half against the Eagles and trailed, 14-0. It was the last regular-season game, and I guess we weren't terribly motivated. We had already clinched a playoff spot but couldn't improve our position no matter what we did against the Eagles.

But we had also lost our two previous games. The last thing the coaches wanted was to enter the playoffs with a three-game losing streak. But there we were, absolutely stinking up the joint. We could tell Bunsy was getting ticked on the sidelines.

So we went into the locker room with all the coaches in the "slow burn" mode. You have to understand that Bunsy normally didn't do any ass-chewing or give any "rah-rah" speeches at

This might have been the first day it *really* sank in that I was a member of a Super Bowl championship team—the day Joe Gibbs presented us with our rings for Super Bowl XVII.

halftime. Usually it was more: "Here's what we did wrong. Here's what we need to do."

This time he was ready to knock some heads. Usually, the coaches go into their own room, and then the assistant coaches come out and address the units separately. Joe Bugel was usually the henchman on offense and Richie Petitbon on defense. As usual, the coaches went into their room, but then we heard a big crash. We found out later Bunsy threw a chair.

They came out of the coaches meeting and Gibbs brought everybody together. He told us how poorly we played and announced to the starters, "You guys think you're leaving the game early? You're going to play the entire game."

He probably thought this would get us motivated, that maybe we'd all jump up and yell, "Let's go kick some ass (or buns, if you prefer)." Instead we just sat there going, "Yeah, yeah, yeah." That's when he lost it.

He was so worked up his voice went up an octave or two. He screamed, "I'VE HAD IT WITH YOU GUYS" and then he punched the blackboard—BAM!!! "I'M SICK AND TIRED OF THIS!" BAM—he punched the blackboard again. This time the blackboard went flying; chalk scattered all over the place.

Bunsy kept on screaming. The vein in his neck stuck out. I thought he would bust something. Joe admitted after the game he nearly hyperventilated.

We went out and outscored the Eagles 21-0 in the second half to win the game. After the game, we walked out of the locker room with the usual assortment of wraps or ice packs. Even Bunsy had a wrap on his hand. He had fractured a bone on the knockout punch to the blackboard.

◆ ◆ ◆

In his early days in Washington, Joe Gibbs and the other coaches used to walk around Redskin Park and say, "Hi, I'm Dick Vermeil. I work 22 hours a day."

Vermeil is one of the legendary coaching workaholics, so our coaches loved poking fun at him. Gibbs later turned into a Dick Vermeil. During the season, he'd spend many a night—all night—watching films or working out the game plan. He would become so wrapped up in his mental preparations, you didn't know which Joe Gibbs you would encounter. One minute it was, "Hi, how are you doing? How's the family?" The next minute he'd just walk by you in a daze as if you weren't even on the planet.

Dexter Manley used to call him "Sybil" after the TV movie based on a true story of a woman who suffered from a multiple personality disorder. Think about that for a second—Dexter Manley making fun of someone with multiple personalities.

One year, I completely ducked Joe Gibbs. I got tired of guessing which Gibbs I would encounter. For about three months, if I saw Joe coming down the hall, I'd jump into the closest room or go down the stairs. If I heard Joe coming up the stairs, I'd go around the corner and wait.

I know it was silly—really childish—but it started to become a game with me. Joe eventually figured it out and said something to Joe Bugel, the offensive line coach. Buges sat me down in his office and asked what the hell was going on.

"Because the guy's crazy," I told him. "You'll see him three times in a row and won't get a word out of him, and the next time it's like you're long-lost friends."

Bugel told me to cut the crap, so my ducking days ended. It was fun while it lasted.

◆ ◆ ◆

Joe Gibbs had a bit of a superstitious streak. The night before and the day of a game, Joe wanted everything the same each week—no deviations.

On the road, we always stayed at a Marriott hotel. The nights before home games, we always stayed at the Dulles Airport Marriott. We always had the same thing for pregame, prenight meal—hamburgers, French fries, and ice cream. The morning before the game, it was the same thing—pancakes, spaghetti, bacon, sausage, eggs, fresh fruit, and cereal. Joe wanted everyone to know what to expect—no changes, no surprises.

Bunsy was also superstitious about flights. We would always arrive the day before a game at approximately the same time—no matter where we played.

Some routines aren't such a good thing. For about two years at the Dulles Marriott our pregame entrée was not only hamburgers every time, it was *burnt* hamburgers every time. It became a running joke.

One of the guys would predict, "They can't be any worse than last week," and have to admit later, "I was wrong."

Finally, we couldn't eat any more of those "hockey pucks." We started throwing the little carbon patties around. We weren't going to eat them. They tasted like garbage.

Buns went off, but this time he took our side. He ran back into the kitchen and chewed out the cook. He started yelling and screaming at the guy about how we're the Washington Redskins, how we stay at the hotel before every home game, and how we should at least expect something edible. The pregame cuisine improved after that.

Two of our assistant coaches, Jerry Rhome and Don Breaux, used to sneak food back into the room. For some reason, they had this thing about hoarding food. Even when we had our Friday barbecues or meals catered in by the Alpine Restaurant, they'd take a plate of food back to their offices or load up one for home. (The Alpine Restaurant, on Lee Highway in North Arlington, is owned by Ermanno Tonizzo and features the best Northern Italian cuisine I've ever eaten. It is still my favorite restaurant in the D.C. metro.) That continued at the pregame meal until one of them tripped on the way back to the room and scattered food all over the place.

After that little mishap, Buns put a stop to the pregame doggy bags.

◆   ◆   ◆

Joe Gibbs was extremely competitive no matter who we played. But there were three coaches whom Joe especially enjoyed beating: Tom Landry, Bill Parcells, and Buddy Ryan.

Joe probably wouldn't admit it, but I got the feeling he had a genuine dislike for Buddy Ryan. With Landry and Parcells, it was more a matter of respect—respect and practicality. In the early '80s, the Cowboys were the team to beat to win the NFC East. When Parcells took over in New York, the road to the division title usually went through New York.

The 1986 season probably best illustrates that. We lost four games during the regular season, one at Dallas, one at Denver, and two to the New York Giants. We avenged the Dallas loss later that season, 41-14. Denver, who beat us by only one point at Mile High Stadium, went on to win the AFC Championship.

After beating the Rams and Bears in the playoffs, we got one more shot at the Giants. They shut us out, 17-0, and followed that up with a Super Bowl victory over Denver.

Do the math. We were 14-2 against the rest of the league that year, but 0-3 against the New York Giants.

◆   ◆   ◆

When Gibbs first got to the Redskins, we started having meetings for the Fellowship of Christian Athletes. Only a handful of guys would show up at the beginning. When Joe started going to the meetings himself, more guys—particularly the older guys—started showing up. I guess they thought they could extend their lifespan with the Redskins. Eventually the meetings were packed. Guys who used to go out and party with the Hogs even ended up in the FCA meetings.

Go figure!

THE STAFF

We had nicknames for all the coaches. I told you about Joe Gibbs and "Buns" or "Bunsy." Most of the others were some variation on their names. Joe Bugel was "Buges"; Larry Peccatiello was "Pec"; Richie Petitbon was "Bone."

Offensive coordinator Dan Henning had a unique nickname. We called him "Vapor Lock" for his frenetic operation of the film projector.

The film machine had buttons that you pushed to run the play back and forth. The night before a game, we knew if Dan Henning ran the projector, a 15-minute meeting would turn into a one-hour meeting. He'd mash his thumb down on that "Play" button and then switch to "Reverse" with equal vigor.

Dan would run the same play over and over and over. After a few repeats, there was nothing new to see. The coaches always thought they were making some great point. The players couldn't have cared less. We got bored quickly.

So we started keeping count. I think 29 was the official "Vapor Lock" record—29 times Henning showed the SAME play, back and forth, back and forth. When the simple count lost its appeal, we made a game out of it. We'd sit around in the back of the room and give odds. For instance, the over-under would be 22—anything to help pass the time.

◆   ◆   ◆

Our film sessions could be brutal. We still had the old-fashioned film projector, and all you could hear in the dark room was that "tch, tch, tch..." as the film passed through the gate. When Joe saw something he didn't like—which was frequently—he'd turn off the projector. There would be this very brief moment of silence, and then he'd let us have it big time.

Joe was a technician and a perfectionist. If your "hat" placement was in the wrong spot or you took a wrong step; if you didn't arm pump on this play or went the wrong direction on that play—anything. If we made a mistake, he'd make sure we'd pay the price.

The film was stored in those big, round, metal canisters. Usually, about the fourth time Joe turned off the machine, we knew we had to duck. He'd start firing those canisters all around the room. Some of the younger players tried to sit in the back of the room, hoping he wouldn't notice you in the dark—but he caught onto that. He made all the rookies and new players sit up front. You'd be clobbered upside the head with a film canister at least once or twice your rookie year.

That may sound a little drastic, but Joe's obsession with detail helped me realize what it takes to be an NFL lineman.

◆ ◆ ◆

The coach I had the most direct contact with was our offensive line coach, Joe Bugel. Buges was the "Boss Hog," the man who named "The Hogs." The hog christening happened during our 1982 mini-camp. Buges decided his offensive line candidate looked like a bunch of hogs.

"Okay, you hogs, let's go down to the bullpen and hit those [blocking] sleds," he'd say.

By the time summer training camp rolled around, Buges had purchased "Hog" T-shirts for us. We had ten charter members in The Hogs: me, Russ Grimm, Joe Jacoby, Jeff Bostic, George Starke, Fred Dean, Ron Saul, tight end Donnie Warren, and John Riggins, the only non-lineman in the group. Tight end Rick "Doc" Walker later joined The Hogs. Of course, Doc wanted to be part of just about every group—The Hogs, The Fun Bunch. I wouldn't be surprised to hear that Doc lobbied to join the Smurfs.

Gradually, the media and the fans started using the line's nickname. As we started piling up victories during the 1982 season, Redskin fans started showing up at RFK Stadium with their own Hog T-shirts and complemented those with Hog noses. It turned into a cottage industry for us. We—The Hogs—even incorporated the name.

Winning, of course, was the key. No funny or clever nickname is going to go very far without getting the job done on the field. After winning Super Bowl XVII, I think the entire Washington metro area went "Whole Hog."

I can say with all modesty that "The Hogs"—as a group—remain the most well-known offensive line in NFL history. The league has produced a number of offensive lines that deserved greater recognition—the Packers in the '60s, the Steelers in the '70s, and the 49ers later—are just a few that readily come to mind. In my humble opinion as an offensive lineman, no team can win a championship without—as Keith Jackson would say—"those big 'uglies' doing the job up front."

The NFL has produced a number of famous defensive lines like The Fearsome Foursome, the Purple People Eaters, or the Steel Curtain. However, no offensive line—as a group—is as easily identifiable as The Hogs. Yes, Buffalo had The Electric Company, but the focus was still on O.J. Simpson (they "turned on the juice").

From 1983 to 1988 Grimm, Jacoby, Bostic, and yours truly collectively made ten Pro Bowl appearances. When the Washington Redskins, as part of their 70th anniversary celebration in 2002, selected the 70 greatest players in franchise history, all five of the original interior starting Hogs—Starke, Jacoby, Grimm, Bostic, and I—made the list.

So as Hogs, we owe a great debt to Joe Bugel, not only for bestowing that wonderful nickname but also for helping mold us into the one of the best and most productive offensive lines ever. We all liked and respected Buges, but there were a few times we were ready to fry his bacon.

We always seemed to play at Tampa Bay in the preseason, and we all hated it. Nothing against the city or the area, but it was usually the last or next-to-last game in the preseason. We weren't terribly inspired; we just wanted to get out of there and start the season. Plus, it was always extremely hot and humid.

One particularly steamy night in Tampa, the starters couldn't wait to get out of the game. No one wanted to get hurt

This was a typical scene during a game—Joe Bugel (left) giving us an earful on the bench. That's Kenny Huff's arm (pleading his case, no doubt).

or nicked up going into the regular season. As a result, we played like crap. We couldn't run the ball. We didn't protect the quarterback. Probably worse in Buges's mind, we didn't seem to care.

We went back to the locker room at halftime, sat around eating oranges and drank some Gatorade while the coaches were in their meeting room. After their meeting broke up, Bugel came out and called us into the shower. We thought that we had misheard him perhaps, so we just sat there looking at each other.

"Get your fucking asses back in the shower. I want to see each and every one of you fucking guys RIGHT NOW," Buges yelled.

We went back into the showers, and Bugel started walking around, pointing in everybody's face.

"I don't give a fuck who you are. I don't care if you're a starter or a backup. This fucking horseshit is ending right now. You may think you'll kick my ass, but I'm gonna fucking put my foot up your ass—each and every one of you. Anybody wanna go at it right now?"

We looked at each other, ready to draw straws for the honor. We were pissed. He was calling us out, questioning our manhood. Fortunately, for Bugel, and our future careers in the National Football League, none of us ever accepted the offer.

The Hogs were offered numerous endorsements for pork products. I can't understand why an underwear ad wouldn't fly. Standing (left to right): Rick Walker, Don Warren, Ken Huff, George Starke, me, Jeff Bostic, Russ Grimm, and Joe Jacoby. Kneeling: Boss Hog Joe Bugel.

Buges continued: "You're all gonna go out there, and you're gonna fucking play, and you're gonna play hard. And if there's anything you gotta say about it, we're gonna end it right now, and we're gonna fucking throw down right now. Any of you guys wanna fucking throw down right now?"

At this point, we were practically holding each other back. He basically called us a bunch of cowards and chicken shits and wanted to take us on, one at a time. Are you kidding me?

After the game, on the team bus and on the plane trip back, we all laughed our asses off about it. And you know what? We did play better in the second half.

◆   ◆   ◆

Coaches will try almost anything to get a team fired up for a game. Our first playoff opponent following the 1983 season was the Los Angeles Rams. The Redskins coaching staff probably thought we were a little overconfident. We had finished the regular season at 14-2 and set an NFL record for most points scored by one team in a single season.

So before the game, Joe Gibbs related a comment that Rams coach John Robinson supposedly made to his team on the team flight after they beat Dallas the week before: "We can break the Redskins like glass."

Robinson's remark got our attention, but that isn't what *really* set us off....

The coaches also told us the Rams' players had come in the night before and urinated on the field at RFK Stadium. I don't know if it was true, but that's what they told us: the Rams' players urinated on *our* field, desecrated the sacred turf at RFK.

True or not, the Rams paid the price. We absolutely annihilated them. By halftime we led 38-7. John Riggins rushed for 78 yards in the first two quarters while Joe Theismann completed 13 of 16 passes for 250 yards.

The final score was 51-7, the largest playoff victory margin in franchise history. Riggo finished with 119 yards and three rushing touchdowns. Theismann ended up completing 18 of 23 for 302 yards. We didn't allow a sack the entire game.

The defense was equally dominant. The "Wrecking Crew" held Rams running back Eric Dickerson to only 16 yards rushing. That same guy rushed for more than 1,800 yards as a rookie. His longest gain against us that day was a mere four yards.

When the coaches graded our game films for the Rams game, even Joe Bugel, the perfectionist, could find little fault with us.

WHEN IN RHOME

Our quarterbacks also benefited from some great coaching. When Dan Henning left in 1983 to take the head-coaching job in Atlanta, the Redskins hired Jerry Rhome as quarterbacks coach. Before joining the Redskins, Jerry was the offensive coordinator in Seattle. He's the guy who convinced the Seahawks to trade for Steve Largent.

Jerry had been a super-stud quarterback in college in the mid-1960s, probably a generation ahead of his time. At that time, the pass was something most college teams saved for third-and-long with an occasional deep throw just to keep the defenses honest. Coaches used to say, "There are three things that can happen when you throw the football, and two of them are bad."

Jerry helped change that way of thinking. He set 17 NCAA passing and total offense records at SMU and Tulsa. In 1964, he finished second in the Heisman Trophy balloting to Notre Dame's John Huarte in one of the closest Heisman races of all time. Jerry got an early baptism to the passing game. He played high school football for his father and threw from a "Pro-T and shotgun formation."

Jerry finished college a few years before the NFL-AFL merger, so the two leagues were still in bidding wars for the top college players. The AFL Houston Oilers offered Jerry a whopping $106,500 and a car—for *four* years. Instead, he signed with the Dallas Cowboys and spent the early part of his pro career playing behind Don Meredith and Craig Morton. Jerry told me that he nearly signed with Houston because he desperately wanted that car. Initally, the Cowboys wouldn't kick in with a car. That held up the deal.

Jerry was with us for five seasons. We screwed with him every year at training. Jerry loved to ride his bicycle at camp. Year after year, somebody would steal the bike and hoist it up the flagpole in front of the dorms. The perpetrator tied it up so high that Jerry always had to use a ladder to get it down. I don't know who pulled that stunt, but my money is on Dave Butz.

THE TRAINERS

A serious injury can be devastating to any athlete, but the Washington Redskins had a special aversion to it. As painful as the injury itself was, as frustrating as the lost time might be, nothing was more brutal than our rehabilitation period at Redskin Park.

Our trainers, led by Bubba Tyer, Al Bellamy, and Keoki Kamau, were borderline sadists. They made it so bad, so unpleasant, and so painful during your rehabilitation, hell would have seemed like a good book for some R&R.

When I first came back for rehab after my knee injury in 1989, I couldn't make it through a session without throwing up. Just working on the exercise bike was excruciating.

They just kept pushing, and pushing, and pushing.

Everything they did was the best thing for us in the long run. Our trainers were magicians in terms of what they could do for injured players, but it was pure torture.

We all had the greatest sympathy for anybody undergoing rehab. We never made fun of players in rehab—not even the most well-meaning, harmless joke.

Rehab under the direction of our trainers was unquestionably the hardest, most strenuous, most agonizing thing I've ever endured. Whether he admits it or not, every athlete lives in fear of injury. We weren't afraid of getting injured because of the hurt. We feared the rehab.

JOE KUCZO

One of my favorite "behind-the-scenes" people with the Redskins was longtime trainer Joe Kuczo. Joe began his association with the team in 1953. Joe was one of the first guys in the Redskins organization who earned my utmost respect.

I always made sure Joe taped my ankles, because he always had a few words of wisdom to impart. I learned very early to listen to everything Joe Kuzco said. He was always right. Joe was like the wise old vet you always see in football movies. He had seen it all—been there, done that. Nothing fazed him.

Joe was a fatherly-type who helped me through those dog days in training camp. He always seemed to know the right thing to say. He was simply amazing. Teams that don't have a guy like Joe Kuczo need to go out and find one right away.

Joe was in his seventies, but he could still beat the pants off anybody in racquetball, including yours truly. Keoki Kamau and the other trainers goaded me into a match with Joe.

"May Day, I'm telling you, the old man will kick your ass in racquetball," Keoki told me. He knew I'd take the bait.

Not that I was ever an All-Star on the racquetball court, but I thought, "I'm in my twenties. I'm a professional athlete. There's no way a 70-year-old man will beat me."

Wrong!

Joe kicked my butt all over the racquetball court. We played for about an hour, and I don't think he took more than three steps. He just knew every angle, every shot. He knew exactly where every ball was going and from where it was coming.

He flat-out blistered my ass.

NATE FINE

When it came to Redskin longevity, even Joe Kuczo was a piker next to Nate Fine, the team photographer, film and video director. Nat had been with the Redskins since the inception of the franchise in 1937—back in the days of Sammy Baugh and George Preston Marshall. In his office was a picture of Nate being honored by Eleanor Roosevelt.

Nate filmed—later videotaped—all of our games and practices. I believe he missed only one game in his first 50 years.

If you didn't know them, you'd swear Nate and Dave Butz hated each other with a passion. They used to go at it tooth and nail.

Nate filmed the practice sessions from a man lift to give the coaches an aerial view. Butzy liked to stand at the bottom of the lift and shake it while Nate was upstairs trying to film. Nate never had to look down to see who the culprit was.

"Damn it, Butz," he would scream, "Quit shaking the damn stand."

Butz would yell back, "Screw you, Nate" and shake it some more.

On some of the balmier days, things could get a little toasty for Nate on top of the lift. So we'd fill up a bucket of cold water for Nate to pull up with a rope. Occasionally, Butz emptied out the water, so Nate would get nothing but an empty bucket.

They used to fuss and argue like an old married couple. It appeared nasty to an outsider, but there was tremendous respect, admiration, and love between those two.

THE TURK

The Turk is one of the most feared characters at any NFL training camp. The Turk is the nickname given to the person who delivers the worst possible news: the coach wants to see you; bring your playbook. In other words, your life with that team, and maybe your life in pro football, has come to end.

When I first heard stories about The Turk in NFL training camps, I envisioned a crusty, battle-hardened, tough-as-nails assistant coach who would more or less tell a player to "Come with me, bring your playbook and shut your mouth, or I'll kick your ass."

Our Turk, our bearer of bad news, was Billy Hickman—the antithesis of that image. Billy was a bespectacled older gentleman. He stood about five foot eight and probably weighed no more than 145 pounds. He was a great guy with a friendly demeanor, and a super sense of humor once you came to know him. He was a gentle, kindhearted, soft-spoken guy. Billy's official title was Administrative Assistant and Defensive Scouting Assistant, but he'll be remembered best as "The Turk."

Billy was thoughtful as he could be, given the circumstances. He tried to leave the player with some dignity. He always waited until morning to tell a player, because he didn't want the guy to have a bad night's sleep.

That was a wise tactic for another reason. If you lay that kind of news on some guys in the evening, they're likely to go out, get liquored up, and cause some trouble.

After a few years in the league, Billy told some stories about his role as The Turk. He could never guess how a player would react.

Some guys were so shocked or stunned, they just stared at him without saying a word. Some guys would freak out and trash the room. Some guys would just start crying. Billy said it was totally unpredictable. The guy you thought was the meanest, toughest hombre would be the one who would break down and cry.

Chapter Three

THE PLAYERS

JOE THEISMANN

Joe Theismann was a terrific leader on the football field—
a true general as a quarterback. Joe was also one of the
most accurate passers I've ever seen. I'm not talking
strictly in terms of percentage. Joe could flat out put the ball on
the money and with great touch. He was also one of the best at
throwing on the move, and I say that with all due respect to
another Joe QB from Notre Dame.

Joe was a great competitor, and I don't think people realize
just how tough he is. Joe has a "healthy" personality, and
sometimes that rubs people the wrong way. As a result, I don't
think they realize how tough Joe was. He'd do whatever it took
to win football games.

◆ ◆ ◆

During my second season with the Redskins—our first Super Bowl season—we played the Giants in a critical game at RFK Stadium. Although it wasn't the worst weather I had endured, it was a typically cold, drizzly mid-December day in Washington. Our offense struggled in the first half, and Joe wasn't enjoying one of his pinpoint passing days. We trailed 14-3 at halftime, but it could've been much worse.

We finally put together a sustained drive about midway through the third quarter, moving to the Giants' 22-yard line. Joe Theismann then handed off to Joe Washington on a fake sweep to the right. Washington was supposed to pull up and throw to Art Monk, but the Giants had the play defended.

Washington reversed fields and headed for the opposite end. All of a sudden, someone was running next to him—it was Joe Theismann. For a second, it looked as if Washington might flip the ball to Theismann in a role reversal of his Oklahoma wishbone days.

Instead Theismann stepped up and took out New York's Terry Jackson with a perfect block. Washington waltzed into the end zone for our only touchdown of the day.

Although Theismann took out Jackson, Jackson took a few of Joe's teeth. We had to play the rest of the game with a lisping quarterback. We can look back and laugh now, but it was hard to understand the plays with Joe lisping and whistling as he talked.

We ended up winning that game 15-14 on a Mark Moseley field goal in the closing seconds. It was Mark's 21st consecutive field goal—then an NFL record. Aside from Mark Moseley, I don't think there was anyone happier with that win than Joe Theismann.

Here's a guy—Joe Theismann—known for appearing with his finely tailored suits and perfectly coiffed hair, probably displaying his altered bridgework to the media as he recounted the tale of his "perfect block."

After that, Joe lobbied to be named an "Honorary Hog," but there wasn't a snowball's chance of that. The only "Honorary Hog" was John Riggins. In Riggo's own words, he was "an offensive guard who got lost on his way to the line of scrimmage."

The Hogs had a strict "No Quarterbacks" policy. That didn't stop Joe from campaigning. We gave him his due. It was a great block and a great effort—but one block does not a Hog make.

◆ ◆ ◆

Joe and I became great friends off the field. He's a great guy, and I love him to death. I'd do anything for him. One thing that helped form a bond between us was our mutual enjoyment of gin rummy. Joe loves to play gin rummy and hates to lose. That's the competitor in him. He doesn't like to lose at anything—football, tiddlywinks, or gin rummy.

Unfortunately, Joe thought he was the best gin rummy player God had ever put on the planet. I guess that's typical of Notre Dame quarterbacks, who think they're automatically the best at everything they try.

We used to play on the planes and in the hotels on away trips. Joe hated it when he lost—which was quite often. He couldn't stand losing. He'd just raise the stakes. We'd keep playing, and Joe would keep losing.

As a first-round draft pick, I was able to buy a house with my signing bonus. It was a brand-new house in suburban Virginia but with an unfinished basement. With the money I won from Joe Theismann in my first season, I was able to finish that basement. I put up a plaque on the basement wall that read, "Dedicated to Joe Theismann."

Once Joe didn't have enough cash on him to cover his losses, and he didn't like to write checks. I knew Joe was good for it, but I cut him a deal. Joe had a big-screen TV in his basement, which was fairly rare at the time.

"If you pay me 'X' amount of dollars now AND give me the big screen," I told him. "We'll call it square."

He agreed.

The next day was an off day for us, so I borrowed a truck from the Redskins and took teammate Darryl Grant with me over to Joe's house. I knocked on the door, and his wife, Shari, answered. I told her we were there to pick up the big screen.

"What are you talking about?" Shari asked.

"You mean Joe didn't tell you?" I said. "Well, I guess he's buying you a new big screen, and I'm getting your old one."

Darryl and I proceeded to the basement, picked up the big screen, loaded it into the truck, drove to my house, and added a new item to the "Joe Theismann Basement."

◆　◆　◆

Joe's ineptitude at gin rummy was well known throughout the team, including a little superstition behind it. Joe used to believe that if he lost at cards before a game, he'd go out and play great. If he won at cards, he'd play like crap. I have to admit, there was some evidence to back up the superstition. We went to two straight Super Bowls in 1982-83 and had a combined regular-season record of 22-3. What does that tell you about Joe's gin rummy expertise?

Even the coaches bought into it. Defensive coordinator Richie Petitbon would come up to me and say, "May Day, you gotta beat him. You just gotta beat him."

Now, here's where it gets a little eerie. Probably the best day Joe ever had against me in gin rummy was Monday, November 18, 1985, just before we played the Giants on *Monday Night Football*.

That night Joe broke his leg in what is still the most famous on-camera injury in NFL history. It was graphic and gory. When Joe's leg snapped, it sounded like a gunshot.

In the next issue of *Sports Illustrated*, there was the photo of Joe lying on his back with me looking over him on one knee.

I was hoping for the best, but even then, I suspected it would be a career-ender for him. I was upset—extremely upset—as was everyone else in the stadium. Here was our quarterback, our leader, and one of my good friends, lying on the ground after sustaining one of most gruesome injuries ever.

But I have to also admit that in the back of my mind—way back—I was also thinking, "Who am I going to play gin rummy with? There goes my cash cow."

◆ ◆ ◆

Seriously, I hate hospitals, but I had to go see Joe. Even when he was laid up, it was still the same old Joe. He wanted to play gin rummy, figuring he was on a win streak. I'm not ashamed to say, I had no sympathy. I won my money back.

I owed him one, though. When I first walked into the room, I received quite a jolt. There was Joe, lying in traction, moaning, with blood all over his forehead and cast—or so I thought. Joe's girlfriend at the time, actress Cathy Lee Crosby, had applied a little ketchup to Joe for "dramatic effect."

JOHN RIGGINS

I don't think I need to elaborate the details on the John Riggins-Sandra Day O'Connor incident—the night an inebriated Riggo told a U.S. Supreme Court justice to "Lighten up, baby," and then passed out at the dinner table. That story made headlines across the country. I can't say any of his

Actress Cathy Lee Crosby, TV's original Wonder Woman, dated Joe Theismann for several years. Cathy Lee had a great sense of humor (in addition to her obvious talents). Best right guard ever? She should have seen me at right tackle.

teammates were surprised when we heard or read about it. We experienced the one and only Riggo firsthand.

We were playing a preseason game in the early or mid-'80s down in New Orleans, and Riggins was told he wasn't going to play. So he decided to go party with Ron Saul. They decided to go out and have a few libations on Bourbon Street. Riggo and Bourbon Street is a recipe for trouble.

Riggo sat—more like reclined—in the back of the room. Dan Henning, assistant head coach and offensive coordinator, ran the projector in the front of the room. The lights were off since we were watching films. All of a sudden, we heard "Zzzzzz...."

Of course, it was Riggo in the back corner, passed out and snoring. Nobody said anything—it was preseason. Most of the guys had come to expect something like that from Riggo.

But that just wasn't enough. John apparently woke up from his little stupor and decided he needed to use the restroom—without going to the restroom.

Suddenly we heard another familiar sound: "Psss..." against the wall.

Everybody turned around, including the coaches, and watched Riggo finish his business. He turned and, as if nothing out of the ordinary had just transpired, he plopped back down in the chair and went back to sawing wood.

No coach said a word or did a thing. They went back to business as usual. If any other player had done that, he probably would have been fired, never to see the light of day again in the NFL—much less the Washington Redskins.

◆ ◆ ◆

Wherever Riggo went late at night, someone had to get him to practice the next morning. After a while, that duty was assigned to running backs coach Don Breaux. Every day Don Breaux would have to go over to John Riggins's house, knock on the door, and pick John up to make sure he was at practice and the meetings on time. Don Breaux was a great coach, but his chauffeuring may have been one of the most valuable services he provided.

◆　◆　◆

One night before a playoff game, Joe Gibbs gave us his usual speech. We were staying at the Dulles Marriott outside of Washington, D.C., as we normally did before the home games.

It was the usual stuff, how we need heart, we need character, we need to get the job done, to play to win, we need to go out and play, and how we need somebody to step up.

Riggo stepped up a little earlier than Joe had envisioned. John, as was his custom, had a few pre-meeting cocktails that night. The guy could play his butt off on Sundays; one could never argue that. Saturday nights, even at the team meetings, he was usually three or four sheets to the wind already.

Riggo was near the end of his career and had had enough of the "rah-rah" crap. He stood up—no mean feat itself—and entertained us with his oration:

"I fucking don't know about the rest of you fucking guys, but that fucking guy up there—Joe Gibbs—I'm going to lay it on the fucking line for that fucking guy tomorrow. I don't give a shit if they've gotta take me to the fucking hospital—as they do every fucking week. But I know one fucking thing: I'm gonna fucking put it out on the line tomorrow for him."

With that, a speechless Joe Gibbs ended the meeting and walked out. The next day, Riggo took his usual shots—but not shots from the opposition. Before the game we could hear John in the training room, "Ugh, ugh, aaaghhh!"

That was the sound of John Riggins getting his enema and B12 shots before the game.

As usual, Riggo piled up a hundred-plus yards, and we won the game.

THE HOGS

We loved to play up the "Hog" image and were willing participants for most photo ops, even for some silly ones. Clockwise from bottom left: me (73), Russ Grimm (68), Jeff Bostic (mostly obscured), Don Warren (85), Rick Walker (88), Joe Jacoby (66), and John Riggins.

Russ Grimm

None of us lived up to the "Hog" persona more than my old Pitt teammate Russ Grimm. Russ was a blue-collar working stiff and proud of it.

Sportswriter Paul Attner summed up Russ pretty well in a 1983 *Washington Post* article: "Grimm doesn't read stock reports. He doesn't wear ties. He doesn't yearn to be a business conglomerate. He's comfortable with a six-pack and a fishing rod."

Russ was all football player. A few administrators at the alma mater probably cringed when Russ proclaimed he went to college to play football, period—but that was Russ.

He went to four straight Pro Bowls as our left guard. He probably could have been All-Pro at center or right guard as well. His arms were too short to be a stellar tackler.

He did love his beer. I hosted a Christmas party at my new house in 1982. My basement wasn't finished, so the party was strictly upstairs. However, I iced down a keg of beer and stationed it on the landing between the first floor and basement. Russ turned the landing into his headquarters for the evening. He grabbed a chair and a Hog shot glass (a 60-ounce pitcher) and parked his butt on the landing next to the keg. Except for an occasional trip to the bathroom, we didn't see Russ on the first level all night. Russ wasn't trying to be unsociable. In fact, Russ maintained he had devised the perfect social strategy.

"The keg's on the landing," he reasoned. "Sooner or later, every guy at the party is going to come my way. What better place to meet and greet everyone?"

Perfect Hog logic.

Russ Grimm is currently the assistant head coach and offensive coordinator of the Pittsburgh Steelers. He was a finalist for the Chicago Bears' head coaching position in 2004.

Joe Jacoby

Joe Jacoby was probably the biggest human being I had ever seen up to that point. I've never been a little fellow myself, but I felt tiny next to "Big Jake." Officially, the Redskins listed Joe at something like six foot seven, 300 pounds. I suspected they fudged a little on the height. I *know* they low-balled his weight.

None of the Hogs had what you'd call washboard abs, but we weren't from the Gilbert Brown mold, either. Joe was proportioned better than most guys his weight. He's just a big man—big neck, big shoulders, big bones, just plain big.

When I worked at WJLA-TV during my second season with the Redskins, we had an intern in the sports department named Todd "Beef" Liller. Beef was a student at the University of Maryland. Beef wasn't very tall, but he was a stocky kid himself, as his nickname would imply. He had classes with a few Maryland football players, so he was familiar with big people, or so he thought.

One night Joe Jacoby came to the station for a live on-set interview. We sent Beef to the front desk to greet Jake and lead him to the set. Beef came back to the sports department, shaking his head, and saying, "There's no sense in it. Just no sense in it."

Naturally, we asked, "No sense in what?"

"There's no sense in anybody being that big!"

The first time Jacoby met Joe Gibbs in a private meeting, Gibbs thought he was a defensive tackle. Bunsy told him things like, "You can learn a lot from Dave Butz." Joe didn't say anything, because he didn't wanted to embarrass Bunsy.

That was typical Joe Jacoby. He was probably the most soft-spoken lineman I've ever known, certainly the most soft-spoken Hog. Joe was like Art Monk in that respect. Neither would say much. Joe and Art would just go out and get the job done. Once in a great while, Jacoby would give a little speech to fire us up. We'd just look at him with our mouths open and think, "Man, he speaks."

Joe was another Charlie Casserly find, an unpolished gem when he joined the Redskins, albeit a very large stone. He's another guy who benefited from the tutelage of Joe Bugel. Jake worked hard and had one hell of a career that included four straight Pro Bowls. Russ Grimm is a finalist for the Pro Football

Hall of Fame and deservedly so. I think Grimm's partner on the left side of the Redskins' line should be a Hall of Fame candidate, too.

Joe and I actually go back to our college days. We played each other. At least our schools, Pitt and Louisville, played each other. When Louisville came to play us at Pitt, the Cardinal players walked around Pitt Stadium before the game and asked for autographs, took pictures of the stadium. They were in awe of the stadium and the history behind it. They also appeared to be in awe of us. Opposing players asking for autographs before the game. I still bug Joe about that every now and then.

Jeff Bostic

We used to call Jeff Bostic, "Poppin' Fresh," after the Pillsbury Doughboy. Jeff was the little Hog. To compensate, Jeff wore cowboy boots with two-inch heels to try to get over the six-foot mark.

Jeff was another guy nobody wanted. He initially signed with the Redskins as a free agent. When the Redskins released him, he tried out with the Eagles and was cut there, too. The Redskins picked him up again with the idea he might be useful as a long snapper on punts and place kicks.

Jeff was tenacious. He worked his butt off and made himself into one of the best centers in the league.

The Dutchman

Donnie "Dutch" Warren was one of best blocking tight ends in the league and had a pretty good pair of hands. He caught 113 passes in his first four NFL seasons, including 29 in the nine-game strike-shortened season of 1982. We didn't throw much to our tight end after that, though.

Some people liked to call Clint Didier a tight end, but Clint usually lined up as our H-Back. Dutch was basically a glorified offensive lineman with a tight end's number (85) on his jersey. From 1983 to 1990, Donnie averaged around 15 receptions per season, about one catch per game.

Sometimes Donnie would go two or three games without catching a single pass. The rest of the Hogs loved to bust his chops over that.

I'd say things like, "Damn, Dutch, add seven or eight digits to my number (I wore No. 73), and I'll catch at least one pass."

Donnie rarely had much to say, but occasionally he would complain about not getting more passes thrown his way. He finally got his wish.

Donnie caught ten passes in one game against the Giants. The only problem was we lost the game, 21-10.

"Now you see why we don't throw it to you," we told him. "We finally did, you caught your passes, and we still lost. Quit your bitching."

Dutch spent all 14 of his NFL seasons with the Redskins, who named him one of the "70 Greatest Redskins" of all time. Obviously, his contributions to our success extended far beyond any pass receiving stats.

Don Warren currently works as a scout for the Washington Redskins.

George Starke

When the Redskins drafted him in 1971, he was an unlikely candidate to emerge one day as one of the "70 Greatest Redskins" and the "Head Hog." There was little doubt George was a good athlete. He was the starting center at Columbia University—the starting center for Columbia's *basketball* team. George was on the same front line with Jim McMillan, who later played for an NBA championship team with the Lakers.

In football, Columbia used George mostly as a tight end on a team that didn't exactly dominate the Ivy League. Matter of fact, George was a member of a Columbia team that lost to Dartmouth, 55-0, the most lopsided defeated Ivy League history (I had to throw that in for George's sake).

He then took a circuitous route to fame and glory as a Washington Redskin. The Redskins traded him early in his first training camp. He played for a couple NFL taxi squads, got waived twice, and returned to the Redskins as a free agent in 1972. He spent a good part of that season on the Redskins' taxi squad.

George just kept banging away. He earned a spot on the Redskins' regular roster, and by 1974, he was the team's starter at right tackle. When I arrived in Washington in 1981, George Starke was a fixture with the Washington Redskins but apparently not enough of one to prevent any confusion with me. Almost from the beginning it started when I was out in public:

"Hey, GEORGE, how you doing?"

"Hey, GEORGE, can I have an autograph?

"Hey, GEORGE, how do the Skins look this year?

George is so old … How old is he? When George was a sophomore on the Columbia basketball team, Pete Carill was a second-year head coach at Princeton.

The mistaken identify hasn't stopped. The last time George and I got together, he told me some guy had asked for his autograph only a couple weeks before. Well, not exactly *his* autograph. The guy wanted Mark May's autograph (obviously, a man with good taste).

George said, "I tried to convince him I wasn't Mark May. Finally, I thought, 'To hell with it' and signed your name."

When we played together, Mr. Starke would occasionally take it to another step. In addition to his honorary title of "Head Hog," George was known also as "The Mayor of

Georgetown." He loved to hang out in the Georgetown area of the district.

Every now and then, he'd venture out from his regular haunts and try out a new emporium. If the folks there started to call him "Mark," he'd play along. He would also ring up a hefty tab in *my* name and then leave.

I'd go into one of the spots for the first time—usually on George's recommendation—and the people there would say, "Mark, great to see you. Now, would you mind clearing up your tab?"

You could almost follow the path of George Starke's nighttime activities by the number of tabs he rung up under my name. I'd have bills—couple hundred dollars—in bars or restaurants I'd never set foot in before. I turned the tables a few times, but George still has the upper hand in that department.

Kenny Huff

I was born several years after the death of jazz legend Thomas "Fats" Waller, so I can't claim to be the inspiration for one of Waller's humorous offerings, "Your Feets Too Big." As Waller phrased it, my "pedal extremities are colossal." I wear a size-16 or size-17 shoe (depending on the make and model). That led to my second nickname on the team (after "May Day"): *Footsie.*

Joe Bugel got it started when he yelled during one drill, "Move your tootsies, Footsie!"

I could never shake it after that.

One of the guys who used to rag me most about my feet was Kenny Huff. Kenny joined the Redskins in 1983 after several years with the Baltimore Colts. He fit in right away and became a welcome new member of the Hogs.

I also have to give credit to Kenny for one of the longest running jokes against me.

During one game, I accidentally stepped on Ken's foot in the huddle. Ken let out a blood-curdling scream and shouted, "Damn you, Footsie, and your big feet. I think you broke my foot."

Kenny limped to the sidelines where he discovered he had, indeed, broken or fractured a bone in his foot. For years, Ken loved to tell the story about how Footsie, with the huge gunboats attached to his ankles, *stepped* on his foot and broke it. For years, I would laugh and tell him that he was a pussy, leaving the game with a broken foot. But the truth is, I always felt bad about it.

Ah, the truth—let's get to the truth. The fact is, Ken Huff broke his foot in that game. And another fact is, I stepped on his foot in the huddle. But the ultimate fact is—and this is the most important part—Ken Huff broke his foot on the play *before* I stepped on him.

For about 15 years, he let me believe that I had broken his foot. I used to laugh along with him when he told the story, but I always felt bad about it. He knew I felt bad, but he kept on retelling the tale for more than a decade.

Good one, Kenny—I owe you one.

R.C. Thielemann

R.C. Thielemann joined the Redskins, and the Hogs, in 1985 after eight seasons in Atlanta. R.C. went to three straight Pro Bowls from 1981-83—another great pickup for us.

R.C.'s locker was always next to mine on game days. He was a good dude, but he was also a chain smoker. He was the first player I had seen who chain-smoked before a game.

I enjoy a good cigar on occasion, but breathing in cigarette smoke *before the game* was never high on my to-do list. Sure, we had plenty of guys dipping into their cans of Skoal or Copenhagen, but that was a private thing. I've never heard of

R.C. Thielemann (69) played next to me on the line for several seasons, and he had the locker next to mine on game days. At 272 pounds, R.C. was one of the smaller Hogs. Maybe smoking stunted his growth.

anyone dying from second-hand snuff. Sitting next to someone who's puffing away is a different story. I had to start busting his chops to get him to go smoke someplace else.

"If you don't smoke 'em all the time," R.C. used to say, "it doesn't bother you."

"Yeah," I'd respond, "but you do smoke 'em all the time."

Everyone knew R.C. was the smokestack on the team. Some of the coaches used to bum cigarettes off him before games.

Donnie Laster

Our last pick in the 1982 draft was Donnie Laster, an offensive lineman from Tennessee State. During a game at

Philadelphia, George Starke went down with an injury, so Donnie Laster had to go in.

On the sidelines, Joe Bugel asked him, "Donnie, are you okay, are you okay? Can you go in?

"Yeah, yeah, yeah," Donnie replied. "I can go."

Donnie started looking around the stadium. He had never seen that many people in one place in his entire life.

Right after insisting, "Yeah, I can go, I can go," Donnie leaned over and then barfed right on Bugel's shoes.

Rick Walker

Some things never change. As a member of the Washington Redskins, Rick wanted to be a part of just about every group on the team. As a tight end, Rick was a member of The Hogs. He was an original member of the Fun Bunch. I think he even tried to worm his way into The Smurfs. At six foot four, 235 pounds, Rick would've looked like a Smurf with a glandular condition.

He's still at it, though, only today he'll join anything with a broadcast signal: Sports Talk on WTEM (980 in Washington), NFL on CBS-Westwood Radio One, ACC College Football Game of the Week, Comcast SportsNet. Set a microphone down, and Rick Walker might plunk down behind it.

I have to give Rick credit, though. Probably as much as anyone, he found a new home with the Washington Redskins. He joined the Redskins as a free agent in 1980 after three seasons in Cincinnati. He caught only one pass in his last year with the Bengals.

His pass receptions didn't skyrocket with us; Rick caught only 56 passes in six years with the Redskins. But Rick was much more valuable as a blocker. His acquisition helped facilitate the Redskin formation switch to a two-tight end, one-back set.

Rick came up with a couple big plays in Super Bowl XVII. He had one of the key blocks on John Riggins's 43-yard touchdown run in the fourth quarter. I emphasize "one of the key blocks"—one of the websites marketing Rick as a motivational speaker exaggerates a tad.

He also had a 27-yard reception to start our only touchdown drive in the first half. Twenty-seven yards! That had to be a career best.

DARRYL GRANT

Throughout this book, you'll read how "lucky" or "fortunate" I feel that I've been. Forgive me if sound like the proverbial broken record (damaged CD for our younger audiences), but a number of things fell in place or came together for me in Washington.

One lucky happenstance came when the team assigned Darryl Grant and me to be roommates for our first Redskins training camp in 1981. Darryl and I remained training camp and road roommates for ten years.

Darryl Grant—"World B. Grant"—is a wonderful guy. A Rice University graduate, Darryl is super smart. He came to the Redskins as a center/snapper/offensive lineman. In his first training camp, he was a Hog—even got his picture taken with the Hogs—but Darryl thought he had a better opportunity to play on defense. He also could get along better with the defensive line coach, "Torgy" Torgeson, more so than the vivaciously rabid Joe Bugel. Thus, he made that transition to the other side of the ball. Darryl became a starter on the defensive line—an often underrated starter in my opinion.

During those years in training camp, we used to talk about football, philosophy, life, our families. We leaned on each other when life took sharp turns, and it was a wonderful experience.

When he went to the defensive side of the ball, we remained roommates and friends even though we had to practice against one another.

We used to just sit there and tell stories about other players and how they had the opportunities to play.

I remember talking about Charlie Brown. Charlie Brown was injured his first year and didn't play that well. A number of people wrote him off, but Charlie kept telling us, "I know I can play in this league. I'm better than these guys are; I know I can play with Art Monk and those guys. I know I can. I just need a chance."

He got his chance, and the rest is history. He ended up a Pro Bowl player.

DEXTER MANLEY

One of the most incredible physical talents I've ever seen was Dexter Manley. Dexter had the fastest 40-yard dash time on the team. Think of that, we had the most explosive offense in the National Football League, and our fastest 40-man is a 250-pound defensive end.

Dexter is a good person at heart—he really is. He'd do anything for a friend, and I consider him a good friend. Dexter, though, isn't the most cerebral person you'll ever encounter and probably the last guy who should be abusing drugs or alcohol. Dexter simply loses control.

◆　◆　◆

During our rookie season training camp at Carlisle, I experienced an early warning sign for the future of Dexter Manley. We came back and played a preseason game at home. They gave us a day and a half off, so we decided to stay in

Washington. Dexter, Darryl Grant, and I went to Georgetown to party a little bit.

Dexter had a few cocktails, and in a matter of 15 minutes, he started running around like a wild man, screaming at the top of his voice, trying to take on anybody within a 200-yard area.

Darryl and I "escorted" Dexter out of there, but on the way home, we stopped at a red light. Dexter jumped out of the car and ran into an apartment building. He knocked down the front door and ran through the building, screaming at the top of his lungs.

Darryl Grant and I looked at each other, thinking the same thought: "We've got to find this guy, corral this guy, and get the heck out of Washington before we all get arrested."

We were able to accomplish the task that night, but that little incident didn't bode well for Dexter's future.

◆　◆　◆

One day, Dexter came to Redskin Park out of his mind—absolutely gonzo. He screamed and argued with everybody. Finally he ran out the building, yelled, "I'm done," and jumped into his car.

We heard him squeal out, followed by the sound of a crash. Dexter had run into an 18-wheeler tractor trailer outside of Redskin Park. He damn near decapitated himself in the process.

Lucky Dexter rolled out of the car and ran back into the building.

The police were called to investigate the accident. When they found Dexter, they wanted a breathalyzer and a urine sample.

To this day, we still don't know exactly how Dexter passed those tests at Redskin Park.

◆   ◆   ◆

I went to see Dexter when I was working for TNT Sports. It wasn't strictly a social call—Dexter was in prison in Texas. When my cameraman and I drove up at the prison, a guy with a shotgun came up and said, "State your business."

After explaining our business, we had to go through the normal security checks. They patted us down and made sure we emptied our pockets. The guards brought Dexter in to see us, wearing handcuffs and leg shackles. He was very happy to see me, and he asked the warden if it was okay if he could show us his cell—just as someone else might take you on a tour of his new house.

The warden gave his approval so we went back to Dexter's cell. It didn't hit me until I saw those wires and all those people in there. They had the "okay" inmates in that block—low-profile guys like Dexter—guys who had made some bad decisions in their lives but were not constant threats. Outside the 15-foot barbed wire were the guys with whom you really didn't want to mess.

It finally hit me: "Holy shit. What did I get myself into? What if these guys—even the ones in Dexter's group—said to themselves, 'Hey, we got Mark May and a cameraman. We can cause some real shit now.'"

Everything was actually cool. They'd come up and say, "Hey, it's Mark May. That's the Washington Redskins guy."

I was beginning to wonder if I was bigger celebrity after my retirement *in prison* than I was "on the outside" during my playing days.

What the hell, it's nice to have a following.

The interview with Dexter went well. It was a fun interview—a revealing look inside Dexter Manley. But I don't think I was ever as scared at any point in my life than when it finally dawned me that, "May Day, you're in prison."

ART MONK

Art Monk and I go back to high school—to the New York state high school track and field championships. Art was a sprinter from White Plains. I threw the shot and discus for Oneonta.

Art would never say anything. In the ten years I played with Art, I probably didn't hear him say more than three words in anger or out of excitement.

Art was one of the most dependable receivers who ever played the game. He wasn't real flashy, but he'd go across the middle to make the tough catches. You wouldn't see Art make six or seven spectacular moves after catching the ball, but he was Mr. Steady. He'd never drop a ball. He'd take the big licks and get the first downs.

Art retired in 1995 as the NFL's all-time leading receiver. Jerry Rice has since buried all the NFL receiving records, but heading into the 2005 season, Art still ranked fifth in career receptions (940) and ninth in receiving yards (12,721).

Art has been a Hall of Fame finalist for five years. He should have been inducted into the Hall five years ago. His quiet nature has probably hurt his chances, and that is ridiculous. Art didn't speak much to the media. That was just his way. Art is a very shy guy and always felt uncomfortable talking with the media.

One of the few downsides of our two '80s Super Bowl appearances was Art was injured and couldn't play in the big game. I think some writers hold that against Art—using the warped rationale that since we won without Art, he couldn't have been that valuable. I guarantee you, without Art Monk, we wouldn't have made it to the Super Bowls.

That shouldn't be held against him. Art is a first-class human being. Look at his performance on the field and his contributions outside of football. In 1993, Art and former

Redskins Charles Mann, Earnest Byner, and Tim Johnson established the Good Samaritan Foundation, which serves disadvantaged youth in southeast Washington, D.C.

Go ask any Redskin player from that era to name three players they respect the most, and Art Monk will definitely be one of the three.

◆ ◆ ◆

As I watched Peyton Manning break Dan Marino's single-season record for touchdown passes in 2004, I remembered when Art Monk broke the NFL record for most pass receptions in a season. Manning's record-breaking toss was the winning touchdown in overtime.

Any athlete would prefer it that way—to break the record when it really counts, when it truly has meaning. That's the way Art Monk did it, and I'm proud to say I was on the field when it happened.

Heading into the final game of the 1984 season, Art had 95 receptions for the year—six short of the record set by Houston's Charley Hennigan 20 years earlier in the run-and-gun days of the American Football League. Our opponent that afternoon at RFK was the St. Louis Cardinals, one of the top scoring teams in the league.

At 10-5, we had a one-game lead in the NFC East, but the Cardinals, Giants, and Cowboys all had 9-6 records. We knew if we won, we would wrap up our third straight division title. We knew if we lost, we would most likely end up in the NFC Wild Card game. There was even a remote possibility that we'd get knocked out of the playoffs altogether.

Things went smoothly for us in the first half. Art caught a pair of touchdown passes, and we led at halftime, 23-7. We fully expected to go out in the second half and pound away at the Cardinals and then crank up the Riggo Drill for an easy win. We forgot to factor in the Cardinals offense.

Neil Lomax absolutely lit us up in the second half—25 of 28 for 314 yards—to rally the Cardinals.

Art Monk, though, kept coming up with the big play. He broke the record in the third quarter. It wasn't a typical short-yardage catch by Art—it was a 36-yard gain to set up a field goal. The officials stopped the game and presented the ball to Art. I think he was a little embarrassed at the time since we had some pressing business left. But he handled it as he always did—with grace, humility, and class.

Art finished the game with 11 receptions and 136 yards. His biggest catch of the day was his last. The Cardinals had taken a 27-26 lead, and we faced a third-and-19 at the St. Louis 47-yard line with 2:50 to play.

We called the same play on which Art caught the 36-yard record-breaker. It was called a "Z-Divide," a formation in which Art lined up as a tight end. Art ran 20 yards downfield towards the right sideline. Joe Theismann threaded the perfect pass—he had to, because three Cardinal defenders appeared to have Art surrounded. But Art hauled it in for a 20-yard gain and the first down.

With 1:33 left to play, Mark Moseley connected on a 37-yard field goal for a 29-27 victory. Mark may have scored the winning points, but Art Monk won the game for us that day.

That's not a knock against Moseley, because Mark set his NFL record in similar fashion—when it counted the most. Mark's record-breaker (for most consecutive field goals) was a game-winner against the Giants in 1982, a 15-14 victory in the closing seconds to guarantee a playoff berth.

I was on the field for both records—both very special moments in my career.

GARY CLARK

In some respects, Gary Clark was the anti-Monk. He could go deep and make the big plays. He was a huge playmaker for us.

Gary would not hide his emotions. He would get in arguments with everybody. He'd even scream and cuss at Joe Gibbs and Joe Bugel.

Gary would do anything to win, but sometimes he would just snap. He didn't care.

He'd yell and scream at the coaches on the sidelines, "Throw me the damn ball. Get me the goddamn ball."

The first few times it happened, some of the players grabbed him and pulled him away—but it was like trying to pull James Brown off the stage. We'd drag Gary off, and he'd just keep coming back.

After a while, we just said, "Ah, screw it. Let him go. They can handle it."

In terms of the sideline volume, Gary Clark and Art Monk were like yin and yang.

DOUG WILLIAMS

In 1986, the Redskins acquired the NFL rights to quarterback Doug Williams in a trade with Tampa Bay. We signed him to back up Jay Schroeder and were lucky to get him.

Doug had seen the highs and lows in pro football. Doug was Tampa Bay's first-round draft pick in 1978 after a stellar career at Grambling University. He led the Bucs to the playoffs in 1979, 1981, and 1982, the first three playoff seasons in franchise history. The Bucs didn't have another winning season until 1997. He also had to withstand a great deal of abuse in his early days with the Bucs, due to both his inexperience and his race.

After a couple seasons in the USFL, Doug's NFL stock probably had slipped a little, but he was a great acquisition for us. The Redskins signed Doug as a backup to Jay Schroeder. He didn't play much for his first year, but Doug assumed the starting quarterback job in 1987 when Jay went down with an injury.

Doug put up good numbers during the season—not spectacular but solid. More importantly, he assumed his leadership role and helped guide us to an 11-4 regular-season record and NFC East Division Championship. Even though Jay was healthy, Joe Gibbs made the decision to stick with Doug at quarterback for the playoffs. Nothing against Jay, because I think each was a capable quarterback and leader, but I think the decision to go with Doug was the right move.

As the playoffs began, maybe even before, reporters started asking Doug about the possibility of becoming the first black quarterback to start in the Super Bowl—which is an interesting query, since most of the NFL pundits were not picking us to get to the Super Bowl.

However, we got there—by beating the Bears 21-17, then the Vikings 17-10 in the NFC playoffs.

The frequency and the lunacy of the race questions increased. None of us were immune. One reporter asked me what I thought about blocking for a black quarterback in the Super Bowl—as if there was a difference blocking for a black (or white) quarterback in the Super Bowl, the NFC playoffs, or the regular season.

I don't remember my answer. I wanted to give some smart-ass remark like: "Doug's black? I spend most of my time with my back to the quarterback. I didn't know."

I'm pretty sure that I said something diplomatic. The last thing any of us wanted was to do or say anything that would reflect negatively on Doug.

I can't think of anybody who could have handled the situation better than Doug Williams. He answered the questions calmly, intelligently, and with a great deal of humility. Doug was quick to pay homage to African-Americans like James Harris and Joe Gilliam, who preceded him as NFL quarterbacks.

He didn't talk about those issues with us much during Super Bowl week. There was no need. As far we were concerned, the color of everybody in our locker room was burgundy and gold.

Doug let his performance on the field do the talking and shut up any of the doubters. He led us to a 42-10 victory over the Broncos, passing for 340 yards and four touchdowns, both Super Bowl records.

Nobody could have handled it any better than Doug Williams did.

DAVE BUTZ

Players can be very superstitious, sometimes even more so when you're winning. Dave Butz, Mark Moseley, and Joe Theismann used to ride to the home games together. Dave would pick up Mark and Joe, always in the same vehicle. They always took the same route. Dave always drove. Mark always sat in the passenger seat. Joe always lay down on a bench seat in the van.

"Joe used to lie down and read *The Washingtonian* or *People* magazine to see if there were any articles about him," Butz said.

Early one season, Butzy ran over a dead squirrel on the way to the game. He had a great game, and we won big. He got it into his mind that every time we had a home game; he had to run over a dead animal to have a good game. So Dave would pick up Moseley and Theismann early, and they'd drive around looking for a dead animal carcass to run over. They might take an extra half hour or 45 minutes just to find something to run over.

Dave will swear up and down that the Redskins never, ever lost when they ran over a deal animal on the way to the game. At a charity golf tournament earlier this year, Dave recalled the *coup de grâce* in their road-kill roundup.

NFL Films asked to follow Theismann through his entire game-day routine before the NFC Championship game with Dallas in January of 1983. They wanted to record Joe's normal preparations, exactly as he performed them for every home game. Naturally, Joe agreed—he never met a camera he didn't like.

Dave was worried that they wouldn't be able to guarantee the most unusual aspect of the pregame ritual—a concern he passed on to Bob Tichnell, a good friend from Frederick, Maryland. Here's Dave's account of what transpired:

"I called Bob the night before the game, and he said, 'A friend of mine shot a squirrel a while back, and he has it in his freezer. He was gonna have it mounted. I'll tell you what. I'll take care of it.'

"So the next day we followed our usual route along the Dulles access road with the cameraman from *NFL Films* shooting in the back. All of a sudden, we saw this triangular sign on a wooden post, with wooden feet and a picture of a squirrel on it. The sign said, 'Caution! Squirrel Crossing!'

"Mark and I looked at each other like, 'Did we really see what we just saw?'

"Next, we passed four or five guys standing in front of a van, holding their mouths, trying not to laugh. Right after we passed them, we saw this great big fox squirrel on the road. He was *frozen* in the running position.

"We made a little detour and—bump-bump—ran over him. It was real quiet for a few seconds as we drove along. Then the guy from *NFL Films* clicked off his camera and said, 'I don't think we can show this on national TV.'"

To the best of my knowledge, they never did.

◆   ◆   ◆

Dave Butz was probably one guy on the team who had more publicity for his feet than I did. If I had the gunboats, Butz had the aircraft carriers. Butzy's tootsies were a couple sizes shorter than mine, but he had the widest feet in the NFL—a size triple-E width. He had to wear some kind of steel shank in the middle of his shoes to keep them from collapsing.

Butzy was surprisingly nimble on those feet. He was an all-conference center on his high school basketball team and set an Illinois state record in the discus.

◆   ◆   ◆

Butzy really took the steam out of one of Joe Gibbs's motivational talks. During our playoff days in the '80s, particularly in the early '80s, the weather was always nasty in Washington—cold, snowing, wet, and windy. The coaches used to listen to the players whine about not wanting to practice. Naturally, I was one of the more vocal ones.

The coaches used to get dressed up like Michelin men—eight layers of weather garments: two jackets, vests, long johns, everything you could imagine. They'd waddle around at practice and tell us, "It's all in your mind. Don't worry about it. It's all mental."

So Gibbs used to give this speech—every year, the same speech: "It's all mental, guys. You can overcome it if you're strong enough mentally."

He'd tell us this story about the workers on the Alaskan pipeline. They brought in workers from the Lower 48 to drive the bulldozers and the trucks, but they could only work for about two hours in the cold. They could only get in two hours at a time, then come in for an hour, then go out for two more—very unproductive. Then they had this brilliant idea to hire Eskimos to run the bulldozers and trucks and the trailers. The Eskimos could stay out there all day long. They'd stay out there eight, 10, 11 hours, because they were used to it, and they were motivated to be out there.

"They were conditioned to it," Gibbs would say. "It was all mental. It's all about mental toughness."

One day, a big hand went up in the back of the room. It was Dave Butz, who was hearing the story for the fifth or sixth time.

"What happens if you look across the line and there's an Eskimo playing across from you?"

If memory serves me correctly, that was the last time we heard the Eskimo story.

JOE WASHINGTON

Joe Washington didn't drive a hummer—he was a hummer. Joe was like a little hummingbird on the field, darting from spot to spot. Off the field, he hummed all the time.

He walked through the building at Redskin Park, constantly humming a little tune. His own ears may have been the target audience, but it was loud. I could hear Joe coming from three rooms away. Getting his ankles taped, he hummed. Sitting in the hot tub, he hummed. On the side of the field, he hummed.

I saw Joe on the sidelines at the 2005 Orange Bowl. He had his shoulder in a sling from a recent operation, but other than that, he looked just as he did 25 years ago. He's still in great shape. I don't think he's added an ounce to that small, compact frame.

I stood to next to him for about five minutes. I kept leaning in closer, trying to hear that familiar hum. As soon as I turned to walk away, there it was (melodically): "Hmmm—mmm—mmmm."

It was loud enough to hear on the sidelines at the national championship game. Old habits don't die.

GEORGE ROGERS

George Rogers came to the Washington Redskins in 1985 in a trade with New Orleans. I knew all about George Rogers. We broke into the NFL in the same year. George was the overall No. 1 pick in the 1981 draft after winning the Heisman Trophy. He narrowly defeated my good friend and Pitt teammate Hugh Green for the Heisman.

(I feel compelled to add that the Pitt Panthers spanked Rogers's South Carolina Gamecocks, 38-6, in the Gator Bowl that year.)

George was initially acquired as backfield insurance. John Riggins posted some good numbers in 1984 (1,239 rushing yards and 14 touchdowns), but the club was worried about his age (36) and back injury from the previous season. There were also some concerns about his drinking, which had always been common knowledge but became even more famous with the celebrated Sandra Day O'Connor incident.

Riggo held out of training camp for a couple weeks and then signed a new contract for $825,000, which made him the NFL's highest paid running back. Early in the year, he looked like the old Riggo, but he lost steam as the season progressed.

George suffered through some early injuries and fumble problems but eventually overtook Riggo as the team's rushing leader.

About three weeks before the end of the season, George told the Hogs, "If you guys get me a thousand yards and a 200-yard game, I'll send you all on a trip."

Going into our last game at St. Louis, George was 113 yards short of 1,000. We knew we had a good shot at getting George his 1,000 yards, but a 200-yard game was something else. As far as we knew, no Redskin back had ever rushed for 200-plus yards in a game.

(At the time, the 195-yard game by Mike Bass was listed as a franchise record. Statisticians later uncovered Cliff Battles's 215-yard effort in 1933.)

Thank God that his first carry wasn't an indication of things to come. If that had been the case, George would have been lucky to get two yards, much less 200. The first time he touched the ball, he ran right into my back and fumbled.

The Cardinals jumped out to a 9-0 lead, but we came back to lead 13-9 at the half and eventually took control of the game. The final score was 27-16, but the Cardinals scored a meaningless touchdown in the final minute, which made it closer than it really was.

With the game in hand, we turned our attention to a more pressing matter—George's 200-yard game and *our* trip. As George got closer and closer to the 200 mark, he started looking up at his rushing totals, which were flashed on the Busch Stadium scoreboard. When he got to around 194 yards, he tried to pull a fast one, telling us he was out of breath and getting sick.

"Guys, I can't hang on," he claimed and tried to leave the huddle.

We all looked at each other in the huddle and said, "No, George, no. Your ass isn't going anywhere. We know what you're up to—you're staying right here with your Hog buddies, who love you."

We dragged his butt back into the huddle and made him stay in the game. George finished with 206 yards on the day and 1,093 for the season.

I'll give George credit. Despite his attempt to worm his way out of it, he sent us all on a nice trip during the off season.

MIKE NELMS

We had any number of guys who loved to get after it—members of The Wrecking Crew, The Hogs, big Dave Butz, and Riggo. However, the guy who had to have the biggest cojones on the team was kick returner Mike Nelms. Mike never called for a fair catch on punt returns.

During the 1981 and 1982 seasons, Mike returned something like 80 punts and only made one fair catch. Even that was a technicality. During a game against Detroit in 1981, the Lions interfered with Mike on a punt return. Officially it went down as a fair catch, but Mike never really called for it.

Mike never cared about his punt return average, which is still damn good. All he cared about was advancing the ball for the team. He didn't care whether it was 30 yards or three inches; he just wanted to advance the ball.

You can't fully appreciate what that means unless you've ever been in that position. One time in spring ball at Pitt, head coach Jackie Sherrill put me on the punt return team as a form of punishment—cruel and unusual punishment as far as I was concerned. I wasn't even the primary target, but as I was watching the ball go to the return man, I got *slobberknockered*—laid out. I can't imagine what it would be like to have every guy in a different-colored jersey zeroing in. You have to have an abundance of balls or shortage of brains to do that week in and week out. You're defenseless at that position.

Mike may have formulated his "no fair catch" policy in the Canadian Football League. He played there for three seasons in the CFL before joining the Redskins in 1980. The CFL has no fair catch rule, but return men there have a little more protection. The coverage team has to give the punt returner a five-yard cushion to catch the ball.

His CFL experience aside, I believe most of Mike Nelms's suicidal attitude on punt returns came from the man himself. Nelms could have five guys around him, but he would still field the punt and advance the ball as far as he could.

That's the kind of selfless player you want on your team.

In our second game of the 1983 season, we were tied at 10 with Philadelphia in the fourth quarter. The Eagles punted to Mike, who was standing near our 40-yard line. At least four Eagles had Mike surrounded, ready to bury him right on the 40. Somehow Mike shook loose. He turned that burial into a big return, which set up the go-ahead touchdown. We won that game, 23-13.

Later, special teams player Pete Cronan—another great niche player for us—said at the beginning of Mike's return, all at once he heard three Philadelphia players say, "Oh, no."

Maybe the biggest return of Mike's career—not the longest but the biggest—came in that great win over Dallas in the 1983 NFC Championship game. The Cowboys had just cut our lead to 14-10 in the second half. Mike returned the ensuing kickoff 76 yards. Five plays later, Riggo bulled over Randy White for a touchdown and a 21-10 lead.

DERRICK SHEPARD

I've witnessed some ferocious hits on the football field, but never had I seen anybody laid out where their eyes rolled in the back of their head—not until Derrick Shepard.

Derrick was a wide receiver and kick returner for us in 1988. We were playing the Oilers in the Astrodome, and Derrick took a kickoff right up the middle. Oiler linebacker Eugene Seale came blasting through the middle and just walloped Derrick—laid him out flat. It was like George Foreman whopping somebody. I have never seen anybody take a hit like that—before or since.

Usually when a guy gets a shot like that, he comes around in a couple minutes, but it was lights out for Derrick. He didn't know what planet he was on. After watching the films the next day, Dexter Manley said he'd rather fight Mike Tyson than return kicks.

Derrick suffered a severe concussion and spent a night or two in the hospital when we got back to Washington. Of course, he was almost immediately placed on injured reserve. I don't think Derrick was ever quite the same after that.

We lost 41-17 against the Oilers that day. They physically beat the crap out of all of us, but nobody took the brunt like Derrick Shepard.

SCRAPPY DOO

The Redskins took a chance when they picked Penn State's Larry Kubin in the sixth round of the 1981 draft. Larry would have been a possible first-rounder, but he blew out his knee in the third game of his senior year. In fact, Larry could have played another college season after receiving a medical redshirt. Penn State fully expected him to return and accused the Redskins of exerting undo pressure on him. Even though Larry maintained it was strictly his decision, Joe Paterno was pissed off—he banned Washington scouts from Penn State practices and refused to send players' films to the Redskins. That was not a good decision for the seniors at Penn State. Many of those players spent three or four years at Penn State with hopes of making it to the NFL, and that's how Joe rewarded them? He shouldn't have deprived his players of any opportunities or possibilities because he had a personal pissing match with the Washington Redskins.

As a junior at Penn State, Larry set a school record with 15 sacks and will swear to this day that he got one of those sacks off me. That's impossible since I didn't allow a sack my last two years of college, but he loves to spread that rumor.

We used to run the Riggo Drill during regular season practices as part of our "team periods." We ran the Riggo Drill at the end of our team period—the 40 Gut, the 50 Gut, 60 outside. The drill was designed to get John in condition and focus, but it also became the standing procedure when we had a late lead as the perfect way to take time off the clock and salt the game away.

The best example of how well the "Riggo Drill" worked was the 1983 NFC Championship game against the Cowboys. With a 31-17 lead and only a couple minutes left, we ran out the clock by running the 50-Gut for nine consecutive plays. That's a simple handoff to Riggo behind the left side of our line and right over Randy White.

On the last few plays, Jeff Bostic and Russ Grimm started taunting the Manster. They lined just before the snap and said, "Hey, Randy. Guess where we're going this time?," and then we ran it right over his ass.

Getting back to Larry Kubin and the Riggo Drill: Larry was a talented, aggressive linebacker, but the knee injury set him back. He spent the 1981 season on the injured reserve list. So when training camp rolled around, he decided he would be more than a ragman on the scout team. Larry made up his mind to challenge Riggo in the hole and try to lay some big hits on him.

The first couple times he tried that we thought, "You idiot! This is our prize bull. Are you trying to hurt the golden bull?" We were needlessly concerned.

On the next play, Riggo laid into Kubin—pancaked his ass. Everybody—offense and defense—must've anticipated it. When Riggo popped Kubin, there was a collective "Woooooo!!!" from the entire team.

After that, we nicknamed Kubin "Scrappy Doo." In every Riggo Drill after that, it was a challenge to see which Hog could knock the crap out of Scrappy Doo before he got to Riggins.

Scrappy never broke into our starting lineup. We traded him to Buffalo for a lower-round draft pick just before the start of the 1985 season.

VERNON DEAN

Our first draft pick in 1982 was Vernon Dean, a hot-shot defensive back from San Diego State, who we picked in the second round. He thought nobody could beat him. He thought he was a great athlete. So he challenged me to one-on-one basketball.

"Sure," I said. "But I'm not gonna play for free."

So ... we put a buck or two on the game.

Now, I will readily admit that if we had played five on five, full court, Vernon Dean would have run me ragged, but that wasn't the game or the bet.

This was strictly one on one, with no shot clock or three-second call.

He took nothing but jump shots and threw up a bunch of bricks.

Vernon was about five foot 11, 205 pounds. I was six foot six, 295. He couldn't block my shot, and he sure as hell couldn't reach around me. I just patiently backed him in and laid it up.

After beating him the first time, I said, "I'll spot you nine out of 11. All you have to do is make two."

So I backed him in again. He couldn't stop me; I just muscled him in.

He said, "Let's double it up."

He was like Theismann in gin rummy. The more we played, the more he lost, the more determined he got and the more he lost.

No, I didn't finish another basement thanks to Vernon, but I was able to buy a few cold brews courtesy of our rookie defensive back.

TIMMY SMITH

Running back Timmy Smith of Texas Tech was the Redskins' fifth-round pick in 1987. Timmy was a bit of a gamble. Timmy grew up in the ghetto of Hobbs, New Mexico. He wasn't the sharpest knife in the drawer, but he had a ton of talent and an explosive gear, so the Redskins took a chance on him.

George Rogers was our No. 1 running back that year. Timmy had limited carries. As we were preparing for Super Bowl XXII, it was apparent the George couldn't go physically.

George was plagued by a variety of injuries throughout the season, almost literally from head to toe. He strained his shoulder in our season opener against the Eagles and sprained his ankle in the NFC Championship game against the Vikings. In between, he suffered a strained groin and was hampered most of the season with a sore big toe, which is much more serious and debilitating than it sounds.

But we couldn't tell Timmy—the coaches knew he was an immature player. They didn't think he could handle the pressure if he knew he was to be the starter. He never knew he was going to play as extensively as he did in that game.

But play he did—all Timmy did was run for a Super Bowl-record 204 yards.

The following year we found out the coaches had made the right decision. Timmy's immaturity kicked in—he didn't participate in the off-season workout program, held out of training camp, and finally reported 25 pounds overweight. We cut him late that year or the following season, and he was out of the league shortly after.

The scouts and coaches read this kid perfectly. As long as they kept him in the box, told him what to do—he could've been special.

He was for that one game.

THE TRASHMAN

One of our guys who didn't receive much publicity but whom I respected a great deal was the Trash Man, Nick Giaquinto. Nick wasn't very big and wasn't very fast, but he was super intelligent and did a little bit of everything. He played special teams. He lined in the backfield or at wide receiver. He was a good blocker. Whatever the coaches asked of Nick, he'd give it his all. He was the ultimate role player.

◆   ◆   ◆

We had many niche players, some you may not remember or maybe never heard of, just a bunch of guys who busted their butts to get the job done. Go back and look at the 1983 team photograph, and you'll see guys like Virgil Seay, one of the Smurfs; Reggie Evans, a backup fullback; or Otis Wonsley, a backup running back and one of the biggest hitters on special teams that I saw during my whole career.

Quarterback Babe Laufenburg was another team player. Babe was a big favorite of the fans. Three years in a row, he led us to preseason comeback wins. The Redskins kept cutting him, but he kept coming back.

I don't understand why it's so hard to put together a team in the NFL today. Everybody, or almost everybody, goes after the superstars and the big names. Go out and find the overachievers who can fill their roles, and you'll have a winning football team. Build through the draft, supplement with free agents where necessary. But that doesn't mean that your free agent has to be a high-priced glamour boy. Keep your own players. Why draft a 21- or 22-year-old rookie, train him, and groom him in your system to be a valuable 25-year-old veteran and then let him go elsewhere?

Why go out and get a spectacular back if you have a sub-par offensive line? Build your offensive line first. You'll see teams go out and spend $10 million on a running back and spend the same amount or less on an entire offensive line. Then they'll wonder why the running back isn't producing. Some superstars aren't as super in a new setting.

Look what the Indianapolis Colts did the two years before they drafted Peyton Manning. They drafted offensive linemen in the first round. They didn't have much to show for it in the win column for a couple seasons—which got them the first pick and the shot at Manning. They built the foundation.

Most quarterbacks taken with the first pick get their butts kicked as rookies. Peyton Manning didn't have to go through that. His offensive linemen had taken their licks in the season or two before his arrival, but they were a solid unit for Manning from day one.

I hear people in the NFL say that due to today's free agent market you have to go for the quick fix and look to win in two or three years or fire the coach. Really? Look at what the Pittsburgh Steelers have done under Bill Cowher. He hasn't won a Super Bowl yet, but he's been to the Super Bowl, and the Steelers are consistently in the playoffs.

Better yet, look at the New England Patriots, a team that has kept the Steelers out of another Super Bowl or two. The Patriots have a number of top-notch players but probably not a bona fide superstar in the bunch. They have a host of marvelous niche players, guys who know their roles and do their jobs.

New England's Ted Washington was a perfect example. That man couldn't run a 40-yard dash in a month. Put him on the Patriots defensive line, though, and he'll occupy two offensive linemen almost every play. Ted probably doesn't have the gaudy stats, but he'll plug the hole and keep the guard and center off the middle linebacker, allowing the linebacker to make the play. New England has a host of other role players, guys like Willie McGinest, Ted Johnson, and Troy Brown. We won the same way.

WILBER MARSHALL

After 1987—the year after we won our second Super Bowl—the Redskins signed Wilber Marshall, another of the "great" Chicago linebackers. Marshall's signing was one of the first big free agent deals. It was also one of the biggest mistakes that the coaches, scouts, and administration for the Washington Redskins ever made.

Marshall signed for more than one million a year—just about what the Hogs made all together. Suddenly, we had several guys holding out, including Darryl Grant, Doug Williams, Timmy Smith, and Neil Olkewicz. Marshall got his cool million, but the Redskins had trouble signing everyone else.

We had just won the Super Bowl *without* Wilber Marshall, and they gave up the world (first-round draft picks the next two seasons) to get him. I realize every team must look to improve each year, even Super Bowl championship teams—but you don't have to mortgage the franchise in the process. We didn't need Wilber Marshall, certainly not at that price.

Wilber had five decent seasons with the Redskins. He even made the Pro Bowl in 1992—after four seasons in Washington. But he wasn't the force he had been in Chicago and certainly not worth the money and draft picks used to obtain him.

WILBUR YOUNG

The Redskins picked up defensive lineman Wilbur Young in a trade with San Diego a couple months before my first NFL training camp. Next to Joe Jacoby, Wilbur Young was probably the biggest human being I had ever seen. Officially, the team listed Young at six foot six and 290 pounds, or an inch shorter and several pounds lighter than Joe Jacoby. I had to line up across Young during practice, so he sure as hell looked a lot bigger to me.

He used to steal my lunch. Our lockers were next to each other, and the defense got out of meetings earlier than the offense, so he'd just help himself to my lunch. Young was in his 11th NFL season, so I don't know if that was his way to haze the rookie, or if he was just that hungry.

After a few thefts, I bought a lock, but he found a way to get behind and underneath my locker.

I finally fixed his ass when I sprayed one of my sandwiches with heat balm. Apparently, he wolfed it down before he could get a whiff.

That was the last time Wilbur Young stole my lunch.

WALLY KLEINE

In the second round of the 1987 draft, the Redskins took Wally Kleine, an offensive tackle out of Notre Dame. Wally was big, even by Hog standards: six foot nine, 308 pounds, blond hair, and blue eyes. Kleine looked like an oversized Dolph Lundgren stunt double.

Wally was a great kid from a good family—a very wealthy family—but he couldn't play a lick, not in the NFL.

I believe one of the reasons that we drafted Wally was because his daddy was in the same country club as George Bush—then Vice President of the United States. That was a good connection for the Washington Redskins.

I kind of took Wally under my wing. As I mentioned, Wally was from a wealthy family; his father was a Texas oil tycoon. On draft day, Daddy flew Wally from Notre Dame on the company's Leer jet. Wally looked the corporate part for his first Redskins news conference: navy sport coat, button-down shirt, and a yellow power tie.

Wally was so cheap that he used to collect the beer cans and soda cans from our parties and turn them in for the deposit. That's how frugal he was.

I always tried to get this kid to relax and enjoy himself, but he spent a good deal of his free time picking up half-cent beer and soda cans.

I finally told his dad one day after a game. His father almost cuffed him upside the head.

The local media played up Wally as the next great Hog, but he didn't last long in the NFL. I ran into Wally a few years ago. He's rolling big time now, running his own business. He's still a great guy. He even established a scholarship fund at his old high school.

I wonder how many soda cans contributed to that.

MOE ELENOWIBE

The Redskins' third-round pick in 1999 was Moe Elenowibe, the Outland Trophy winner out of BYU. Moe was from Nigeria, where bathing habits are apparently less refined than here in the United States. You could smell Moe 15 yards away. He had that Mother Nature funk to him. I don't think the man ever used soap if he did take a shower.

Moe was a great kid and a smart kid, but he had that Mother Nature, African-continent funk that told you he was coming around the corner 20 yards before he got there.

Moe played a few seasons in the NFL and, at last report, was still playing in the Canadian Football League.

CURT SINGER

In 1984, I was on the sidelines during a late preseason game when the phone rang. Someone yelled out, "May Day, the phone's for you."

I picked up the phone, and "a voice from above" said, "May Day, tell Curt Singer that he just injured his knee."

Curt Singer was an offensive tackle, our sixth-round draft pick from Tennessee.

"What?"

"Tell Curt Singer he just injured his knee," the voice said.

"Gotcha."

So I walked over to Curt Singer and said, "Curt, you're going down on the next play. You're going to grab your knee."

"What the hell are you talking about, Mark?"

"Read my lips," I said (later a popular phrase in Washington). "If you want to be on this team this season, you're going to do it on injured reserve. Go down on the next play."

On the next play, he went down, but he didn't just grab a knee—he started floundering all over the ground. It was one over-the-top performance. Everyone—the trainers, players, coaches—everyone knew he wasn't hurt.

Our head trainer, Bubba Tyer, a little disgusted, went out on to the field and said to Singer, "Get off the ground."

Singer continued the act, so Bubba took him to the sidelines. He looked around at the rest of us with an embarrassed look on his face. We just tried to look away and keep from laughing because we knew it was a fake job.

A couple days later, the rookie who "just injured his knee" went on injured reserve with a back injury.

WILLARD REAVES

In 1988, the Redskins signed running back Willard Reaves from the Canadian Football League. Reaves was a former CFL Player of the Year, and the Redskins inked him to a big signing bonus.

Despite his success in Canada, it became apparent very quickly that Reaves was not NFL-caliber. However, since he got such a big signing bonus, the coaches and the front office were afraid to cut him. They knew Mr. Cooke would go ballistic.

The result: a replay of the Curt Singer incident.

Late preseason game. Sideline phone rings.

"May Day, it's for you."

The voice: "May Day, tell this running back that he's gotta pull a hamstring or twinge a knee. He's going down in the next series."

"Gotcha."

I had to be the world's largest telephone receptionist. I delivered the message to Reaves, but he wasn't quick to comply.

"I'm not doing it," he said.

My response: "Look, I personally don't give a shit what you do, but if you want to remain with this football team and GET PAID this year, you're going grab a hammy or grab a knee on your next series. You're going down if you want to be here."

On his next play, Williard Reaves grabbed a hammy and rolled around on the ground. The trainers came out and helped him limp off the field.

Guess what? A couple days later Willard Reaves went on injured reserve.

Reaves eventually played in the NFL. He had one career carry for a negative one yard.

MORE DEXTER MANLEY

Dexter had to be the most gullible guy on the team. Dexter also enjoyed the spotlight and loved to talk with the media. Naturally, the Hogs took advantage of those personality traits.

On several road trips, one of us called Dexter's room and pretended to be a reporter. A typical script would read like this:

"Hello, Mr. Manley. My name is Paul Bingyuns. I'm a reporter for the *Arizona Republic* newspaper, and I would love to do a feature article. Unfortunately, I only have today to do the interview. If you have time, I will be happy to meet you in the lobby in about 20 minutes."

Dexter dressed up in a suit and went down to the lobby to accommodate the eager journalist. Occasionally, Dexter got a legitimate call from a reporter, which made it easier to pull off our scam. He bit on it every time—hook, line, and sinker. He never caught on. He would sit there for about an hour before giving up.

For some strange reason, Dexter got a seat on the New York Stock Exchange. He tried to play the part. Dexter would dress up in a nice business suit and walked around with an expensive leather briefcase. Dexter carried two items in that briefcase: his lunch and the *Wall Street Journal*. He ate the lunch but never read the *Wall Street Journal*—not really.

If Dexter opened up a newspaper, he was strictly faking it, compensating for his inability to read. Think about this. Dexter spent four years in college. He was graduated from Oklahoma State University—but he couldn't read, at least no better than your average second-grader.

He used little tricks to get by. He'd have people read his press clippings to him, saying he loved the sound of someone else's voice reading his name. At a restaurant, he'd never order first. He'd pretend to read the menu, and then piggyback on another person's order: "I'll have what he's having."

When Joe Theismann broke his leg in 1985, Dexter finally realized his football career wouldn't last forever. To his credit, Dexter started taking classes at night to learn how to read. In 1988, he testified before a Senate committee on illiteracy.

Dexter has made some bad choices in his life. Ultimately, he's the one who has to accept the responsibility and pay the price for those choices, and he has paid a price.

But Dexter had some help along the way.

How does a guy get into college, much less graduate, when he can't read beyond a second-grade level?

Who's taking responsibility for that?

Chapter Four

THE OPPOSITION

HOWIE LONG

Of the teams I faced on a regular or semi-regular basis while with the Redskins, I'd list the Giants and the Bears as the most physical opponents. As an infrequent opponent, the Raiders—with the likes of Lyle Alzado, Reggie Kinlaw, and Howie Long—score high on the "most physical" charts.

Howie Long and I entered the NFL in the same year. Howie, from Villanova, was the 20th pick in the second round of the 1981 draft—exactly one round after me. We didn't face each other on the field until our third seasons, but my experience with Howie Long goes back to a few weeks before the draft.

This was a few years before every team converged in Indianapolis for the NFL scouting combine—the annual cattle call in which departing college players are subjected to a series of physical and mental tests for pro scouts and coaches. In 1981, the league staged a series of mini-combines in various cities.

Howie Long and I went to the combine in Tampa. We hung out a little that weekend—just sat around and shot the breeze in our underwear (they strip you down to next to nothing for the tests). At the time, he was a little rough around the edges— street rough from growing up in the tough Charlestown section of Boston. He definitely was not the smooth Howie Long you see today.

I didn't know too much about Howie before that meeting in Tampa. We had played college football in the same state, but Villanova wasn't exactly a powerhouse in the East. In fact, the biggest news to come out of Villanova football just before the 1981 draft was the announcement that the school was dropping its football program (reinstituted a few years later as a Division I-AA program).

I do remember that Howie was pretty arrogant and cocky at the combine. Apparently, he had a basis for his "confidence." He obviously impressed the Raiders' scouts. Still, if you had told me that some guy from Villanova named "Howie" would be a future NFL Hall of Famer, I would've bet my signing bonus and given you pretty good odds.

Howie Long and I met on the football field for the first time when the Raiders visited RFK stadium on October 2, 1983, in one of the greatest regular-season games of my career. Although we lined up on the same side of the line, we weren't lined up directly across from each other. I was at right guard and Howie was at left defensive end. Our right tackle, George Starke, faced Long most of the time.

Imagine my surprise when, after the second play of the game, Howie Long started yelling at me. I went back to the huddle and asked George, "Is he cussing at you or me?"

George, who seemed almost as surprised as I was, said, "He's yelling at you, May Day."

"This Howie Long is deranged," I thought. But, I figured if he was going to yell at me, I might as well get my shots in.

After the game, he whined loud and long to anybody who would listen, especially to the reporters who were all too happy to pass along his comments.

"I was beating him like a drum all day," he was quoted as saying about me. "And all he could do was hold me or cheap-shot me."

Howie did register four sacks that day but beat *me* like a drum? As I already pointed out, I wasn't the one lined up against him.

We both might have been practicing for future careers in broadcasting, because I joined in the verbal sparring after the game. When informed of Long's comments, I referred to him as a "jerk" and essentially intimated that he had no class.

Did I cheap-shot him a few times? Damn straight. But I wasn't the only one. There were a number of penalties called for unsportsmanlike conduct, and there could have been more. Howie Long was nailed with a flag or two if memory serves me correctly.

I enjoyed the comments from his own teammate, linebacker Matt Millen.

"So what, anyway?" Millen told the *Washington Post*'s Michael Wilbon. "Mark May pushed me in the back once. But it's not like I never push anybody in the back. Anyway, the fights were fun."

The game had to be a lot of fun for the fans, especially the hometown crowd at RFK. We led 17-7 at halftime but trailed, 35-20, with seven minutes left in the game. With 33 seconds to go, Joe Washington caught a little duck pass from Joe Theismann and made a great move at the goal line to score. We won, 37-35.

That game had a little bit of everything. The Raiders scored on two plays of 90-plus yards. Cliff Branch caught a 99-yard touchdown pass from Jim Plunkett. Greg Pruitt returned a punt 97 yards for another Raider touchdown (who fields a punt on his own three-yard line?).

The two teams combined for 890 yards (459 yards by the Redskins—not exactly a major victory for Howie Long and the Raiders' defense). We even got a little lucky on a successful onside kick with six minutes to play—successfully recovered but not according to the way we planned.

The game was draining, emotionally and physically. George Starke called it the roughest individual game he ever played.

Rick Walker and I both suggested the game could serve as a great Super Bowl preview. Of course, Doc and I went from prophetic to pathetic when the Raiders dusted us in Super Bowl XVIII.

◆ ◆ ◆

Before the Super Bowl, a few reporters dredged up the October postgame quotes from Howie and me (as broadcasters today, Howie and I would probably do the same thing). Fortunately, neither of us took the bait. We both shrugged off our previous comments as "heat-of-the-battle" stuff and didn't add any more fuel to the fire.

Just about everybody—the fans, the media, the coaches, the players—believed Super Bowl XVIII was going to be a classic. The Redskins and Raiders were the best teams in pro football. Both were exciting, flamboyant, and physical—Goliath versus Goliath. Instead, we looked like David without his sling.

A number of my friends and family members were in Tampa. After the Raiders clobbered us, they were all upset—some even crying. Naturally, I wasn't in my best "let's party" mode, but I tried to be the cheerleader.

"What's there to be so sad about? I'm 23 years old," I said. "I've been to two Super Bowls in my first three seasons and won one last year. Be happy. Maybe we'll get a rematch next year, and we'll win that one."

We didn't get the Super Bowl rematch, but I faced the Raiders and Howie Long two more times as a Redskin. In 1986, we beat them again at RFK Stadium. The game was lower scoring but no less physical than the previous regular-season matchup. We trailed most of the game but finally prevailed, 10-6.

We scored the winning touchdown on a three-yard touchdown run by George Rogers behind Raleigh McKenzie and me—right over Howie Long. Raleigh had lined up as an extra tight end. We double-teamed Howie and knocked him right on his ass, paving the way for the game's only touchdown.

I hot-dogged it after the play. While the others celebrated the touchdown, I just stood there and pointed to Howie Long in the prone position.

After the game, the imminently quotable Howie Long told the *Washington Post*'s Christine Brennan, "They say holding's an art, and today, R.C. Thielemann was Picasso."

R.C. Thielemann? I was hurt.

Little did I know that three seasons later—on October 29, 1988—I would play not only my last game against the Raiders in a Washington uniform but also my last full game as a Redskin.

The week before the Raider game, I broke my wrist against Tampa Bay. I played, but not that well. We self-destructed in just about every way imaginable—eight turnovers. The Raiders beat us, 37-24, and Howie Long definitely got the better of me that day. I can't attribute that totally to the broken wrist—but it certainly didn't help.

Today, I get along great with Howie Long. Any of our past altercations—physical or verbal—were just part of the game and in the past. Howie is a bona fide Hall of Famer. I wish I could have faced him more often.

LAWRENCE TAYLOR

The two greatest players I ever faced—bar none—were Lawrence Taylor and Reggie White. I never wanted to see Lawrence Taylor line up on my side of the field. He was so quick that you could knock him down on the ground, and he'd still get up and get to the quarterback. He was relentless, one of the most relentless players in the history of the game.

Every time L.T. came over to my side, I would gouge his throat or go after his stomach. I didn't try to injure him, but I did want to hurt him—at least enough to get his attention. We wanted to know exactly where Lawrence Taylor was at all times. We designated him the "Rover"—Rover Right or Rover Left, depending on where L.T. lined up. Lose track of L.T., and you were likely to lose yardage on the play.

Every time L.T. came to my side, I tried to hurt him. I wanted him to reach the point where he did not want to be on my side, because I sure as hell didn't want him there. I knew I was going to lose sooner or later. You take a 295-pound lineman backing up while trying to fend off a 245-pounder—with a 4.5-second 40-meter dash—running towards him, and you can bet the big guy will lose eventually. I wanted to make damn sure that when he came over to my side, he didn't want to come back.

L.T. and I went back to our college days. We played against each other when he was at North Carolina and I was at Pittsburgh. I knew at that time that he was a tremendous athlete, but I didn't know how good he was going to be once he got to the next level. I don't think anybody did. We lost to L.T.'s Tar Heels, 17-7—our only loss in an 11-1 season. North

Carolina forced eight turnovers. As you may have guessed, L.T. was a major factor.

L.T. was like another Tar Heel—Michael Jordan. Most basketball experts predicted Jordan would be *a* star in pro basketball, but I doubt anyone penciled him in as *the* star, possibly the greatest basketball player of all time.

Once Lawrence Taylor got to the NFL, he opened eyes and turned heads. As great as he was in college, it was amazing how much he improved in his first year in the NFL. That might have been the biggest leap ever in one year as far as performance level. He was incredible in college, but once he started playing under Bill Parcells, he turned into a different animal.

DISHIN' THE DIRT

An executive in the National Hockey League once said, "There's more violence in one football game than there is in an entire hockey season, and nobody ever talks about that."

Well, let's talk about it. The area between the sidelines in a National Football League game is a violent world. Unless you've played the game or even stood on the sidelines at an NFL game, you don't have a full appreciation of how big the players are, how fast they move, and how viciously they collide. Watching the game on television or even from the stands will partially sanitize the brutality of the game. Oh, you'll watch the big hits on the highlight films, usually out in the middle of the field— a linebacker nailing a running back, a safety cold-cocking a receiver. But it's also a tremendous physical game in the trenches. Every snap is like a violent explosion.

Kenny Huff, who played alongside me on the Redskins' offensive line told me a story about the first time he got a sideline pass *after* he had retired.

"I had only been out of the game a couple years," Kenny said. "I stood there and couldn't believe it, how hard they were hitting. I thought, 'I can't believe I actually did that.' Just two years removed, and it already seemed like a different world to me."

There's a lot of *chippiness*—cheap shots, trash-talking, eye-poking—that fans rarely see or hear. And I must confess that I have some dirt under my fingernails. In fact, I had a reputation as one of the dirtiest players in the NFL. I wasn't like Conrad Dobler, who had the dirty reputation in the media. Dobler loved to fan those flames. Mine was, for the most part, strictly inside. My thought on that was, "Why call attention to it? Don't throw up a red flag to the gentlemen who throw the yellow flags."

Our coaches frequently had to put a muzzle on Dexter Manley. Before a game with the 49ers, Dexter essentially told the media that he was going after Joe Montana, one of the league's golden boys. Now, I'd never consciously suggest that I would overprotect Joe Montana or anyone else. The number of concussions Joe sustained in his career is a testament to that. But if Dexter Manley put a hit on Joe Montana that is marginally late or flagrant, whom do you think would get the call?

So I kept it low key with the media and the public. But I didn't mind if word spread through the players' grapevine.

One year the Atlanta Falcons had a first-round pick—I believe it was Mike Pitts, a defensive end from Oklahoma—who was scheduled to line up across from me. As we walked into Fulton County Stadium, he walked up to Kenny Huff and asked, "Is that Mark May really as dirty as he looks on film?"

When Kenny told me that, I knew I had him. Before the game even started, I was inside his head.

I got my early indoctrination into the underbelly of pro football against the Dallas Cowboys, which probably comes to no surprise to Redskins fans. Randy White and I—from my rookie year on—couldn't stand each other, even though we rarely played head to head. I look back at it now as fun, but we used to really get into it. At the time, it was pure hostility.

We hated each other.

We took every opportunity to give each other a cheap shot. I'm not talking about trying to blow out each other's knees or inflicting some other type of serious injury. I mean the little extracurricular "love taps"—at the bottom of the pile, getting up from the pile, 20 yards away from a play, when your back was turned. I expected it against the Cowboys. I expected it from Randy White. He taught how to play dirty in NFL. He taught; I learned.

I remember one play against the Cowboys when he pushed me in the back. While getting up from the pile, I *may* have stepped on his hand—by accident, of course. As I was walking back to the sidelines, I saw Ron Saul waving for me to turn around. Randy was coming at me in a dead sprint, apparently intent on nailing me in the back. I whirled around just as I hit the sidelines. Randy stopped, flipped me the *double bird* and then trotted back to the sidelines.

◆   ◆   ◆

When I moved from left tackle to right guard, I no longer lined up across from Randy, but I still got my licks in after the play. Randy started taking it out on Russ Grimm, and Russ got pissed at me. Once we got into a big argument right in the huddle, which is a major faux pas—only the quarterback talks in the huddle. Finally, Joe Theismann had enough of our bickering and screamed, "Will you guys shut up?"

Joe finally had to call a timeout to straighten us out.

◆ ◆ ◆

It wasn't just Mark May and Randy White, though. Overall, the Washington Redskins and Dallas Cowboys genuinely hated each other. During the 1984 season, we had a mid-December game in Dallas. As usual, emotions were pretty high. We overcame a 15-point halftime deficit to take a 30-28 lead and got the ball back in Dallas territory with about a minute to go.

Joe Gibbs was concerned we wouldn't run out the clock if our quarterback, Joe Theismann, simply took a knee. So he told Theismann to kill some time. Joe ran back and danced around a little before taking the kneel-down. This really pissed off the Cowboys. They already considered Joe to be a big "hot dog" anyway. They claimed he was trying to rub it in when all he did was kill some time—as instructed. One of their defensive backs, Ron Fellows, barreled in, and laid a cheap shot on Joe from behind.

Naturally, I went after Fellows. While I was grabbing him, somebody grabbed me from behind—it was Randy White. A big fight ensued, and the officials finally had to call the game with 24 seconds remaining. The next day I read in the papers that Randy White wanted to meet me in the parking lot.

The parking lot? Randy, I was right there on the field. Don't tell the media in the locker room. Tell me when you have the chance. But that was typical of my matchups with Mr. White.

JOHN DUTTON

I always thought Cowboys defensive tackle John Dutton was a big stiff. I couldn't tell anybody that, though, because Dutton usually lined up across from me.

Starke had Too Tall Jones, Jacoby had Harvey Martin, Russ had Randy White, and I had John Dutton.

I'd tell those guys how great Dutton was, and they'd say, "Bullshit. He's never been to the Pro Bowl with the Cowboys [Dutton went to three Pro Bowls as a Baltimore Colt following the 1975-77 seasons]. Look at the other three guys."

Who knows? Dutton may have tried to make the same case with his fellow linemen.

BIG BUBBA

Al "Bubba" Baker, a six-foot-eight defensive end for St. Louis, was the Moe Howard of the NFL—the head Stooge without the sound effects. Baker had a penchant for poking the eyes of offensive linemen—down in the pile, on a pass rush— anywhere he could slip that digit into your eyeball.

"Don't pull that crap on me," I told him before one game. "Poke your finger in my eye, and I'll put a size-17 shoe up your ass."

He was a good little Bubba until halfway through the second quarter. Then he poked me right in the eye. That was it. From that play on, I stepped on his fingers, poked him in the ribs, and kneed him in the back. If he turned around to break on the ball, I'd turn around, find him, and ear-hole him every single play until he quit.

By the end of the second quarter, Big Bubba was screaming and crying to the official about the things I was doing to him. I didn't say a word to him. Bubba folded his tent and didn't come out for the second half.

Like Little Jack Horner, Big Bubba couldn't keep his finger out of the pie. A couple years after our mix-up, when Baker was with the Vikings, he received a game's suspension for poking the eye of Eagles lineman Ron Heller. Later that season the NFL slapped Bubba Baker with a $10,000 fine for a late hit on Bears quarterback Mike Tomczak.

I loved to get inside an opponent's head—talk to them, give them a couple cheap shots—just enough to get them off their game. I usually knew when to pull out of it before they got too ticked off or they threw a punch. If an opponent did throw a punch, I very rarely threw one back. The retaliatory shots are usually the ones the officials see.

In 1985, we were playing a tight game against the Steelers at Three Rivers Stadium. Keith Willis was at defensive end for the Steelers, and we were going at it a little. We starting knocking each other around, giving each other a little extra shove or shot. The *chippiness* soon escalated.

With about 40 seconds left in the first half, I got Willis with another quick shot at the start of a play. The play ended in an incomplete pass, but Willis turned and nailed me after the play. The official standing right in front of us didn't see it. Ken Huff came over to help, and he and Willis got into a shoving match. I grabbed Kenny around the arms and tried to hold him back as he and Willis started jawing at one another. By this time, we had the official's undivided attention. As I was holding back Kenny, Willis—in full view of the official—swung and hit Kenny right in the facemask. Out came the flag, a 15-yard penalty on Pittsburgh.

That allowed us to kick a field goal just before halftime. We won the game, 30-23.

I got a big chuckle out of Willis's quote the next day in the paper:

"*Mike* May was doing it," Willis said. "Huff came over, I guess he figured *Mike* May could hold his own."

Please, Keith. I went to college in Pittsburgh. Get my name right.

THE GIANTS

Any time we played the New York Giants, we knew we were in for a physical game—The Hogs against Lawrence Taylor, Carl Banks & Company.

Banks was on my side the majority of the time. One game, we started going at it—a little shot here, a little shot there. On one play, he turned around and spat. The "loogie" hit my arm. I don't know if he even realized it hit me, but I went off. I tore after him, shoved him, and spat in his face.

Carl went freakin' ballistic. Two or three guys held him back while he screamed, "I'll kill you. I'll kill you."

All the time he tried to spit at me, but nothing came out. He was yelling so hard that no sound came out of his mouth. That pissed him off even more.

Rest assured, Carl got me back before the end of the game.

◆ ◆ ◆

Most of the time, that stuff stays between the lines. When you walk off the field of play, you don't carry it with you. You forget about it and move on.

DA BEARS

I only faced the Chicago Bears a half-dozen times as a Washington Redskin, but I have several vivid memories from that rivalry. The game I remember most was a playoff matchup at Chicago following the 1986 season.

The previous season, the Bears won the Super Bowl in dominating fashion. They finished the 1986 season with a 14-2 record. They didn't look quite as devastating as the 1985 Bears, but they were heavy favorites to beat us in the playoffs.

The Redskins weren't chopped hog meat. We finished the regular season at 12-4, placed second in the NFC East, and beat the Rams 19-7 in the NFC Wildcard game. We understood why the Bears were favored, but we were beginning to get a little peeved with some of their pregame comments. And when we stepped onto Soldier Field, something happened that really got us going.

The Bears had some kind of awards program before the game, and all of the wives were down on the sidelines in their mink coats or various furs—dressed to the hilt. The "Super Bowl Shuffle" was playing on the PA system while the wives were laughing and talking about their Super Bowl plans. As we warmed up, we could hear them talking about where they were going to go and what they were going to do in Pasadena (site of Super Bowl XXI).

We already believed that we could win, but that really pissed us off. We beat them 27-13 after outscoring the Bears, 20-0, in the second half—yeah, 20 second-half points against the vaunted Bears defense.

I sincerely hope their wives got their room deposits back.

◆   ◆   ◆

My first game against the Bears on October 11, 1981, was special in many ways. It was not only my first win as an NFL player but also Joe Gibbs's first victory as an NFL coach. Our win in Chicago didn't exactly send shock waves through the league. We were 0-5 heading into the game. The Bears dropped to 1-5 after the loss.

Looking back, though, that was the beginning of something special for the Washington Redskins. Counting that win, we won 36 of our next 43 games and went to a pair of Super Bowls.

That game in Chicago represented another first for me— the first time (of several) that I broke my nose. I had to go back in when Joe Jacoby suffered a sprained neck in the fourth quarter. Victory has a way of soothing the pain.

◆   ◆   ◆

Another sweet victory over the Bears was our playoff win in January of 1988, another game at Soldier Field. We fell behind 14-0 but came back to win, 21-17. What really stands out in my mind is Darrell Green's punt return—an incredible effort by Darrell. He hurdled a couple Bears and tore a rib cartilage in the process. He ran the final 30 yards holding his rib cage. That gave us a 21-14 lead and proved to be the winning score.

That victory was significant for a couple reasons. It was the first playoff step in the march to the Super Bowl, where we beat Denver, 42-10.

It was also the final game of Walter Payton's career. The last play for Walter in pro football was a fourth-down swing-pass reception in the last minute. He picked up seven yards, but we stopped him one yard short of the first down.

I'm sure millions of football fans outside the Redskin Nation were hoping Walter would produce one more little burst of magic. Hell, I would've been rooting for him, too, if I hadn't been on the sidelines.

I'm not breaking any ground to say Walter Payton was one of the greatest players and finest persons to ever grace a football field.

◆   ◆   ◆

In *The Way We Were*, Barbra Streisand sings, "What's too painful to remember, we simply choose to forget." That sentiment must not apply to football. I'll never forget our 1985 regular-season game at Soldier Field, one of the worst defeats in Redskins history.

The Bears chewed up many teams that year, and they thumped our butts, 45-10. We actually took a 10-0 lead when

Wayne Sevier, our special teams coach, decided to call out Willie Gault on the kickoff.

"We're gonna kick to his ass and see what he can do with it," Sevier told our special teams unit.

We kicked it to Willie all right, and our coverage team saw his ass—saw it getting smaller and smaller as he streaked right by our guys—99 yards for the touchdown. To make matters worse, Jeff Hayes tore a thigh muscle on the play. Jeff handled the kickoffs for us, but his most important role was punter.

We didn't have a capable back-up punter, but we had one guy who thought he could fill the bill. Once it was clear Jeff was out of the game, Joe Theismann kept pestering Joe Gibbs on the sidelines. I swear he lobbied more than a senator pesters the president to pass a bill.

Anybody close to him could hear Joe saying, "I can punt. I know I can do it."

On the next fourth down Gibbs gave in; he really didn't have much choice. The only positive aspect of Joe Theismann's first NFL punt is that the ball hit his foot. The ball went straight up, into the headwind, and right back down. Officially, the punt netted 36 … INCHES—one whole yard.

I didn't catch the hang time on that one, but we were all ready to hang Joe. We just eye-balled him all the way off the field. Gibbs, tightlipped, flashed him a glance that said, "Geeeez! Just go sit down some place and shut up."

Then Jay Schroeder, Theismann's backup at quarterback, got the call as Joe's relief punter. Jay failed to evoke memories of Sammy Baugh kicking the football, but his first punt was an improvement over Theismann's—a whole 22 yards. At least Jay kicked it past the first-down marker.

In my opinion, we had a better option. Russ Grimm punted at Pitt and did well. Russ was good athlete. He played quarterback in high school, and some major schools recruited him at that position. Now there's one hell of an emergency quarterback. I can picture Russ, six foot three, and 295 pounds, taking the snap behind five-foot-11, 280-pound Jeff Bostic.

Why not complete the trifecta? Insert six-foot-six, 295-pound Mark May at fullback.

You've heard of "Full House Backfield." We could have been the league's first "Full Hog Backfield."

◆　◆　◆

On second thought, I'd just as soon not carry the ball if it means running at Mike Singletary. That game in Chicago marked the first time I remember seeing stars—those circular stars that whirl around inside your noggin. Singletary nailed me right under the chin and absolutely knocked the crap of me. Now I know how a boxer feels when his legs go to jelly. I almost passed out on the field.

Of course, being smacked by Mike Singletary doesn't exactly put me in a select group. Mike was without a doubt one of the greatest football players I ever played against, and without question one of the hardest hitters. Mike defined intensity. He also was great at harnessing his ferocity. Most football fans have seen the clips of Mike just before the play, looking like some bug-eyed madman, followed by his calm, articulate postgame interview wearing those accountant-type glasses.

Mike is now the defensive coordinator and assistant head coach of the San Francisco 49ers. Before that he was an assistant for the Baltimore Ravens. When Mike initially entered the coaching ranks, he offered his services to the Bears. They turned him down flat.

It's mind-boggling that Mike Singletary isn't with the Chicago Bears. Granted, Mike had no coaching experience when he first approached the Bears. That didn't seem to bother the Ravens. He proved his worth in Baltimore—enough to impress the 49ers.

The McCaskey family reportedly didn't want to bring back Singletary, because it would place too much pressure on the organization. George Halas is probably spinning in his grave to find out his descendants would not bring back one of the greatest players in franchise history. Insecurity does not win Super Bowls.

I realize the best players don't always make the best coaches, but Mike Singletary is not some loose cannon. He's a man with a great intellect and a proven ability to motivate.

To me, there are only three Chicago Bear icons from the 1980s. Yes, I know there were a number of popular players and coaches from those teams; but there are only three I consider true icons: Walter Payton, Mike Ditka, and Mike Singletary.

Don't tell me about Dan Hampton. If Dan Hampton is an icon, he's an icon for the overrated. The fact that Hampton is in the Hall of Fame with a player like Singletary is a farce. I'd like to lease the kneepads Dan Hampton used to get into the Hall of Fame—I'd be making a trip to Canton, too. Of all the defensive tackles I faced in my career, I wouldn't put Dan Hampton in the top 15.

I read an interview with Hampton in which he claimed Joe Gibbs told him that we designed our game plan to double team him. I'm sorry, I must have missed that meeting, and so did the other Hogs. During my ten years with the Redskins, only two players were double-teamed by design—Lawrence Taylor and Reggie White.

Dan Hampton? That's a laugh. Hampton was perhaps a serviceable defensive tackle—but he was not a player who put fear in our hearts, certainly not one we had to double team. If we were going to double any of those Bears, it would have been Singletary or Richard Dent.

The fact is, against the Bears' famed 46 defense, our blocking scheme called for gap blocking, or swoop blocking. There is no way you can double-team *anybody* in that scheme.

If I could've lined up against Dan Hampton every week, I would have gone to the Pro Bowl every year.

THE AURA OF AL

As we prepared for Super Bowl XVIII against the Raiders, our coaches were positively paranoid about Al Davis and how he might spy on us. Our practice sessions were closed. Any time there was a body within eyesight, practice was stopped. If a plane or helicopter flew over, practice was stopped. I think we got too uptight worrying about Al Davis and his alleged spies. It took away from our focus and preparations for the game.

One time they spotted a guy taking a photo from about three buildings away. They stopped practice pronto. They accused the guy of spying for Al Davis.

You would have thought we were the Germans protecting the U-2 plans from the British in World War II—that our game package for the Super Bowl was that top secret. I believe that's one of the reasons it blew up in our faces.

I met Al Davis a few times as a player and had conversations with him on the sidelines. I've also talked with him after my retirement. Al always knew everything about me. He knew what I did during the season, what I had done in prior seasons. That's another reason why many players want to play for the Raiders at some point in their career. They have an owner who knows the game. He still is one of the brilliant minds in football. When I spoke with the guy, if I ran into him at some function, he knew everything about me. He's one of the few owners who really knows the game.

REGGIE WHITE

I also got a sneak preview of Reggie White in college. I played him head to head when I was a senior at Pitt and he was a freshman at Tennessee. I had the upper hand then, but I could tell this kid would be pretty damn good. He was a tremendous athlete, a high school All-American in both football and basketball.

After a great career at Tennessee, Reggie played his first two years of pro football with the Memphis Showboats in the USFL. When that league folded, he joined the Philadelphia Eagles.

I remember the first time I played him as pro. It was the third game of the 1985 season. I watched him on films and could barely believe what I saw. He just pushed offensive linemen into the quarterback or knocked them off their feet. He was quick as a cat, strong as a bull, and positively relentless in his pursuit.

Meanwhile, Joe Bugel kept trashing Reggie all through the film session.

"This guy's a rookie. He's a USFL reject," Bugel muttered. "He ain't that good. We're just going to line up and knock him around."

All the time I thought, "It ain't gonna happen, Joe. You're right. He's not that good. He's *damn* good."

I reached into my little trick bag for my first pro encounter with Reggie White … I stepped on his hand. I started cussing at him. I knocked him down on the ground and then gave him a shove in the pile.

Reggie would just say, "God bless you. God will forgive you."

That started getting into *my* head.

About midway through the third quarter, I got into a conversation with one of our tight ends, Donnie "Dutch" Warren, on the sidelines.

"Dutch, what's the matter with this guy?" I asked. "I've called him every name in the book. I've tried every tactic I know. The guy just keeps coming and coming. He's relentless every play. And then he wants God to bless me."

"You dumb-ass," Dutch said. "The guy's an ordained minister."

I apologized to Reggie White after the next play.

"Reggie, I'm very sorry," I said. "I didn't know you were a man of God."

"God will forgive you," he said. "God will bless you."

On the next play, the Reverend Reggie White damn near administered last rites. He blasted off the line and drove me back into the quarterback. The Eagles beat us that day, 19-6.

Amen, Reggie.

Later in my career, I figured that the better the player, the nicer you should be. After about two years of banging heads with Reggie White, I tried reverse psychology.

I'd say, "That's a great play, Reggie," or, "I saw you play last week, and you had a great game, Reggie." If he got close to making a tackle I'd say, "Hey Reggie, great effort."

If a guy was that good and I had to line up against him for the whole game—especially the older I got—I wanted to make sure he wasn't flying high the entire game. Instead of playing at level 10, I hoped he'd ratchet it down to a level eight. Even at level eight, Reggie White was better than about 99 percent of the people I faced.

I'm thankful I didn't have to face an opponent of Reggie White's caliber every week—but we can never have enough people around like Reggie White.

His death in 2004 left a tremendous void.

Chapter Five

TALE-FEATHERS

FIRED UP

Once, a *defensive* coach's pep talk actually fired me up.
Just before Super Bowl XXII against Denver, defensive
coordinator Richie Petitbon got up and exhorted his
players, "I don't give a fucking shit how many times you guys
hit Elway or how many fucking personal fouls you get. You hit
him, you knock him down as many times as you can. You get
close to the quarterback, you knock him on his ass. I want his
nose bloody. I want his shirt dirty."

So there I was, an offensive lineman who wouldn't get
anywhere near the quarterback, and "Bone" had me all fired up.

Prior to the team introductions, we were in the same tunnel
leading to the field as the Denver Broncos. The tunnels from
the locker rooms came from different directions but fed into
one big tunnel.

Normally I was quiet right before a game. I tried to use that time to get my thoughts together—to get all my thoughts and energies focused on the game and what I had to do.

This time, I looked at the Denver players, and for some reason, I lost it. I snapped, freaked out. I started pointing at the Denver players, yelling, "Look at those motherfuckers. Look at those little cocksuckers. They've got fear in their eyes. They've never won a fucking Super Bowl, and they never will. We'll kick their fucking asses every single play, those chicken-shit fucking bastards."

As we entered the field, Joe Jacoby turned to me and said, "Calm down, May Day, calm down."

Denver took a 9-0 lead in the first quarter. "You big-mouthed dumb ass," I started to think. "Now they're fired up. They're going to kick our asses."

But we erupted in the second quarter. We piled up the most points in one quarter in Super Bowl history and destroyed the Broncos, 42-10.

That was the most fun I ever had playing football. It was incredible. From the second quarter on, everything worked— every play we ran, every adjustment we made.

Sometimes it almost seemed liked sandlot ball as we'd draw out plays on the chalkboards on the sidelines: "Okay, they're crashing in down at the ends so we're gonna take the Counter Trey outside, guards are gonna fold around the tackle. Timmy Smith, just hang onto the tackles, and you run to daylight."

That's exactly what happened.

Later on it was: "Okay, we're gonna run the play action now. They've got safeties coming up. We're gonna throw the ball down the field. The safeties are biting on the running game. When the safeties come up and bite, throw downfield."

It all worked. They couldn't stop anything. From psycho to sandlot in one quarter—that was a unique experience for me— and it all started with a defensive pep talk.

I have one sidebar to that story. My father was in the stands for that Super Bowl and happened to have a seat in a Denver section. He said all he saw in the first quarter was orange and blue, Denver fans all over the place, chanting and cheering. At halftime, some of those same fans went out, took off their face paint, and came back with Washington Redskins shirts. Maybe I wasn't the only person with a split personality that day.

THE FUN BUNCH

Unfortunately, that game in Dallas marked the beginning of the end for the Fun Bunch. The Fun Bunch had originated the previous year against the Detroit Lions in our first playoff game. The inspiration of the Fun Bunch was Art Monk. Art was injured and out of commission for the playoffs. Several of the receivers, tight ends, and backs wanted to put on some kind of display to honor Art. They decided that when any one of them scored a touchdown, they would all form a circle, spread their arms, and cross them at their chests twice as a show of togetherness. They finished it off with a leap in the air and a group high-five.

Our 31-7 victory over the Lions included three touchdowns by Alvin Garrett, so the Fun Bunch had many opportunities to perform. Our fans at RFK Stadium loved it, and the Fun Bunch continued their ritual throughout the playoffs and the Super Bowl. The Fun Bunch celebration became an instant tradition with Redskins fans. Just like the Hog followers, Fun Bunch fans came to games wearing Fun Bunch T-shirts.

Original Fun Bunch members included Rick Walker, Alvin Garrett, Charlie Brown, Rich Caster, Donnie Warren, Clarence Harmon, and Otis Wonsley.

They decided to keep it going and performed the high-five act at both home and away games. Art Monk even joined in.

Again, our offense provided many opportunities as we scored 27 points in 15 of our 16 regular-season games.

The intent of the Fun Bunch wasn't to taunt or mock our opponents, but the act was beginning to wear thin at some stops around the league. Miami coach Don Shula was among the most vocal in his opposition to on-the-field celebrations, including the Fun Bunch.

Naturally, the Cowboys weren't exactly enamored with the Fun Bunch. Then again, they didn't care much for the Hogs, the Smurfs, the Pearl Harbor Crew, or anything else associated with the Washington Redskins.

They were boiling over when we gave them the major league ass-whooping in the "Camouflage Game." After an Art Monk touchdown, the Fun Bunch squared off to do its thing. Dallas defensive backs Michael Downs and Dennis Thurman got right in the middle and tried to interrupt the proceedings. A small scuffle ensued—some shoving and jawing. Minor stuff in the grand scheme of things, but it provided some extra ammunition to the anti-Fun Bunch contingent.

In the off-season, the NFL owners—in their infinite wisdom—changed the language of the league's anti-taunt rule to include "any prolonged, excessive, or premeditated celebration by individual players or group of players." They didn't specifically mention the Fun Bunch by name, but it didn't take an English professor to decipher their careful wording.

Rules changes are the work of the NFL Competition Committee, headed at that time by Shula and Tex Schramm, the Cowboys' general manager.

When asked to comment on the rule change, Shula deferred to Schramm.

"After all," Shula said, "Tex has seen the Fun Bunch celebrate in the end zone more than I have."

REDSKINS PARK

Redskin Park, which was built in 1971 during George Allen's reign as head coach, was one of the first facilities built exclusively for an NFL team away from the stadium. It was the blueprint for all practice facilities in the NFL.

We had two practice fields, a turf field, and a natural grass field. It was fenced in, but there wasn't high security in those days. Anybody could park in our parking lot. Anybody could walk in the front door. Anybody could walk into the locker room for that matter, although unauthorized people were asked politely to leave from that point.

One of the wiser things Joe Gibbs did was make Redskin Park seem like a second home. At the time, we were probably required to report more than any other team. We were the first to hold the so-called voluntary off-season workouts and off-season condition programming. Joe Gibbs wanted us to be comfortable in that environment. He wanted us to want to be there.

Most teams weren't like that. Their players would come in for their meetings or practices, and then they'd hightail it out of there. Redskin Park was organized in such a way that players wanted to be there.

The relationships with the players were incredible. We knew we could count on each other then, a feeling that even extends to today. I don't know if the NFL will ever see a crew like that again, one with the type of continuity and camaraderie that we had.

RFK STADIUM

We had three buses that took us to RFK Stadium on game day: The early bus, the late bus, and the coaches' bus. I always took the early bus or a cab to the game. I wanted to get there as early as possible so I could begin my preparations for the game. Many of the guys did the same thing. They took cabs. They didn't want to wait in line for tape and then have to rush to get ready for the game. It was always the older players who arrived early, never the rookies. It gave us some time to relax. There was a certain rhythm and flow in terms of game preparations. The veteran players learned that.

At home, we drove our own cars to RFK Stadium. We drove our cars to RFK on game day. My first couple of seasons in the NFL, I was on autopilot on the way to RFK Stadium on game day. I was so focused on the game that everything was a blur.

Then I started to notice things heading down Constitution Avenue and driving around the Capitol. Walking into RFK Stadium was like stepping on to a rickety old battleship. The stadium was built in 1961 and beginning to show signs of age. Some of the concrete was falling down. A few of the metal pipes were rusting. Yet RFK had so much history and character. Plus it was our home—as Washington Redskins players, we took great pride in playing at RFK.

As I walked through the bowels of the stadium, I could smell the coffee brewing, the popcorn popping. When I stepped out onto the field, I loved the smell of the freshly cut grass— *natural* grass, the way it should always be for football. When I stepped out of the dugout to reach the field, I could stick my hand out, and I'd be touching fans. That's how intimate RFK was. In today's age of skyboxes and luxury suites, the stadium environment is so sterile. The players are so far away from the stands. Back then we could high-five the fans as we walked in at halftime or after the game. You can't do that in most stadiums today—unless you have a stepladder. I know part of it is for safety and security reasons, but a good deal of intimacy between the players and fans has left the National Football League.

When we played, people would bring their entire families. We saw a ton of kids in the stands. I don't see much of that today. The families, for the most part, have been priced out of it. The gravy train might be steaming along right now, but it concerns me about the future of the Washington Redskins and the National Football League.

Another regular pregame routine was to look up to the "Squire's Box"—Jack Kent Cooke's private box. As I warmed up, I always wanted to peek over my shoulder to see who was there—which movie star, which politician, or which powerbroker. It was always someone of note, even in the preseason games. It seemed like the bigger the game, the bigger the celebrities. An invitation to Jack Kent Cooke's private box for a Redskins game was a huge status symbol in Washington, the toughest ticket in town.

The most powerful people in the world came to see us play football—quite an ego trip for the players. We'd shake their hands in our locker room after the game. Most of us probably didn't fully appreciate it then. We were too concerned with the game or ourselves.

Now that we're old and retired—well … retired at least— we'll talk about those things when we get together. The consensus is: "Wow, that was cool!"

TEAM TRANSPORTATION

We were treated first class in every respect. We rarely saw an airport terminal. When we traveled, we would leave Redskin Park on private buses that would take us to Dulles Airport. The buses drove through the back gate, right up to the plane—no security, no luggage check, no waiting.

When we returned, it was the same thing. The private buses would pull right up to the plane, pick us up and haul us back to Redskin Park. Teams can't do that today due to the heightened security. Even then, few teams operated that way. When I went to San Diego and Phoenix, the team had to walk through the airport like everyone else. We'd have to get there early and then sit at the airport like everyone else. That was a big shock for me.

I was extremely spoiled as a Washington Redskin.

PRO BOWL

Selection to the Pro Bowl is now a three-pronged procedure. Players, coaches, and fans all get a say. Democracy is a wonderful process, but it's far from perfect. Every year deserving players are kept off the Pro Bowl roster while others are selected due to past deeds or reputation.

I've heard arguments on both sides as to whether the fans should be involved. On one side of the coin, the fans should have a say in who they watch in the Pro Bowl. It helps stimulate an interest in the game, an interest that has declined.

On the other side, there's the argument that the average fan isn't as knowledgeable as the player or coach. Instead of voting on players based on true value or ability, they vote strictly for a "name" player or cast a ballot based solely on statistics, which are often misleading. Others, of course, vote for their favorite players or only for players on their favorite team.

The players and coaches *should* be more knowledgeable, *should* have a greater insight as to who is truly deserving of Pro Bowl recognition, and *should* cast their votes accordingly. Unfortunately, that's not the case, nor has it ever been. In some cases, the players and coaches are less informed than the fans— at least in the way they choose to vote.

When I was in the league—and I'm sure it hasn't changed much—voting for the Pro Bowl wasn't a private, secret ballot.

We had an open discussion in the locker room. We asked some relevant questions like, "Who was the toughest guy you played against this season?" But we also went through some of the same checklists the fans use: "Who's leading in sacks?" "Who's leading in tackles?" "Who made it last year?"

We could only vote for players in our conference, but we didn't play every team in the conference in a given season. I used to get ticked off because our guys voted for players on teams we didn't play. If we didn't play against them, or even watch them on films, why should we vote them to the Pro Bowl?

NFL politics also figured in the voting.

To give you an idea how absurd the Pro Bowl voting can be, consider the fact that John Riggins went to only one Pro Bowl. He never made it as a Washington Redskin. In 1983, he rushed for a career-high 1,347 yards and an NFL-record 24 touchdowns but didn't get a free trip to Hawaii.

Some of our guys got pissed at me because I voted for the player or players who gave me the most headaches. If I had a difficult time blocking an opponent during the year, and if I knew—from watching films—that he had a solid season, I believed he deserved consideration. I never voted for a guy simply because he had been there before, even if he'd been to the Pro Bowl several years in a row.

I felt I could give a fairly honest assessment of the defensive players I played against, especially the down linemen and linebackers. But what did I really know about the performance level of the defensive backs? How could I evaluate any offensive players? Hell, if I had to cover the wide receivers, I would have voted for all of them.

I wasn't disappointed or bitter that it took me eight seasons to make the Pro Bowl. To the contrary, I appreciated it more— I was honored, and I took it very seriously. I was voted in in a year the Redskins had a losing season, Joe Gibbs's first losing season. That meant more to me, because it meant somebody was paying attention. I wasn't elected on prior reputation or because I rode the wave of a championship team. When I got to Honolulu for the game and all the related activities, I enjoyed it much more.

THE HOGETTES

When the Hogettes first arrived on the scene, we were a little embarrassed to be associated with them. We thought they were a bunch of goofballs. These were grown men who put on women's clothes—dresses, wigs, hats—with their Hog snouts. We never tried to take ourselves too seriously but wanted to protect a macho image of the big, tough offensive linemen. Snouts and skirts didn't seem like a good combination.

Then we found out most of these guys worked for the federal government, either as lawyers or aides for top government officials. So these guys weren't quite as goofy as we originally thought. We met with them and discovered they were all pretty cool. The Hogette routine was just their way of supporting the Redskins and the Hogs.

Earlier this year when I heard the identity of Watergate informant "Deep Throat" was revealed, I was almost afraid to check it out for fear he was also a Hogette.

As silly as they look in full Hog drag, this group is serious when it comes to their work for charitable organizations. Since their formation in 1983, the Hogettes have raised millions of dollars for a number of charities, including Children's Hospital, Ronald McDonald House, Joe Gibbs's Youth for Tomorrow, and Darrell Green's Youth Life Foundation.

Check them out at: www.hogettes.org.

THE MAN-LIFT AWARD

Nate Fine was the regular resident atop the man lift, but he wasn't the only one to reach the summit. For a season or two, we had the "Man Lift Award." If you were chosen Player of the Week, you got to stand on the lift platform, we'd raise it to the top, and you got your picture taken.

Guys took pride in that. I know it sounds like utter stupidity for pro football players to get a charge from something like that. Those little incentives—the Man Lift and Leather Ball awards or the Parking Spot for the Day—were sources of pride.

There was usually a small monetary award, like a hundred dollars—a nice little stipend back then. Now if you offered a hundred bucks to a guy, he'd probably laugh at you. Today a team is lucky if it can get most of the players to come in for voluntary off-season workouts for three or four thousand dollars a week.

CHRISSIE'S ANGELS

I'm not ashamed to admit that two of my favorite celebrity encounters in Washington were Chris Evert and Cheryl Ladd. I spent most of my NFL career in the world's most powerful city, where I had the opportunity to meet and greet national, even world, leaders. Yet, I remember "the babes."

In 1988, the Washington Touchdown Club honored Cheryl Ladd with the Hubert H. Humphrey Award for her humanitarian contributions. As impressed as I was with that, I may have also been slightly influenced by the fact that I always considered her the hottest *Angel*. Sorry, Farrah.

I made damn sure I met her at the Touchdown Club dinner. She was striking, even more beautiful in person than on

Darryl Grant (center) and I were proud to present tennis star Chris Evert with a Redskins jersey. Chrissie would have been one of my top draft picks.

television. We talked for a while, a very pleasant conversation. We had a nice little rapport going, I thought.

Later, as I stepped up to the dais to give my speech, someone handed me a note and told me it was from Cheryl (I felt I was on a first-name basis by then).

The message was short and sweet. One word, four letters: KISS.

I was pumped—big time.

Then I turned it over and it read: "KISS—Keep It Short, Stupid."

I still don't know who sent that message. I prefer to tell people I got a kiss from Cheryl Ladd.

At another Washington function, I had the opportunity to meet the Queen of Tennis, Chris Evert. Chris, like Cheryl Ladd, was even better looking in person. In fact, I thought Chris Evert was even hotter than Cheryl Ladd. Seriously, it was no contest. I give game, set, and match to Chris. She was *smokin'* hot. She also had a dynamite personality. I wish I could have spent more time with her (and I mean that in a nice way).

One of my duties was to present Chris with a Washington Redskins jersey with a No. 1 on the back.

Tough job, but somebody had to do it.

GLENN BRENNER

Glenn Brenner was the funniest guy I have ever seen on television. I don't mean the funniest sportscaster. I mean the funniest *person* I've ever seen, locally or nationally.

Glenn was the sports director at Washington's CBS affiliate.

More people in Washington sat around waiting for Glenn's five-minute sportscasts than Johnny Carson. We knew Glenn would say something funny that we'd be able to chat about the next day. Tapes of his sportscasts are probably long gone. I wish I had the rights to those. I'd put them on a DVD and sell it in the Washington metro area.

It was no act for Glenn. He was as funny off the set as on— maybe even funnier. Glenn was a pretty fair athlete in his day. He even pitched minor league ball in the New York Mets organization. He reported the major sports stories but never took sports or himself too seriously.

He kept me in stitches any time I was around him. There aren't that many people who can do that all the time. I'd put Glenn Brenner in my top three as far as people with whom I enjoy hanging. He was incredibly good-natured and always had a positive attitude. He could make me laugh just by looking at me. He had that effect on everybody.

We all gravitated toward Glenn Brenner. If he came out to Redskin Park for an interview, most guys would try to slide over just to listen to him, because you knew it would be funny.

Glenn also co-hosted the *Redskins Sidelines* show with Sonny Jurgensen. All the guys wanted to be a guest on that show because it was such a blast.

The station sent a limo for the player-guest, and you'd arrive about an hour before the show. The standard procedure was to head over to a nearby restaurant, the "Dancing Crab," for a great meal and a few libations. You'd go back to the station, record the show, and then head back to the Dancing Crab, where you stayed until about one in the morning.

Highlights of the *Redskins Sidelines* included the special football "prognosticators" Glenn brought in to challenge Sonny's picks, everything from a nun to a chimpanzee.

In a review of *Redskins Sidelines* in the *Washington Post*, Norman Chad wrote:

"The show's saving grace is the presence of Brenner, who could spend the entire 30 minutes acknowledging the crowd's opening applause and make it work."

Sadly, Glenn passed away in 1992 at age 44. He is sorely missed.

McHOGS

The Hogs did a commercial for McDonald's, part of the hamburger chain's "I Got a Taste for McDonald's" campaign. We had to perform a few dance moves for the spot, so they had a special instructor to choreograph the pigs' feet dancing in front of the Capitol building and in a local McDonald's.

A few of the Baltimore Orioles—including Cal Ripken Jr. and Eddie Murray—joined us in the spots. The ad agency put together three spots, one with just the Orioles for the Baltimore market; one with just us for the Washington area; and a combined spot for both cities.

When the commercials aired, whose feet do you think they used on the close-ups? It was none other than Footsie's tootsies,

Okay, so we weren't the Rockettes, but the Hogs got a chance to kick up their heels while filming a commercial for McDonald's. From left to right: me, Joe Jacoby, Don Warren, George Starke, and Rick Walker.

and not because my size 17s were the biggest. I had the sweet feet.

It's been 20 years, and I still can't get that damn jingle out of my head:

> *I've got a taste for McDonald's;*
> *That's where I really should be … oh, oh, oh!*
> *I've got a taste for McDonald's;*
> *Only McDonald's—McDonald's—for me.*
> *I've got a taste for only one place;*
> *I've got a taste for McDonald's!*

THE FIVE O'CLOCK CLUB

Our infamous shed in Washington was a building at the end of the practice facilities. After practices, the offensive line and a few others—Riggo and maybe a few defensive linemen would gather for the "Five O'clock Club." No quarterbacks were allowed in this exclusive fraternity. Punters? Hell, they couldn't even find the building.

"One more and I'm outta here" was our motto. We had it printed on hats: "Five O'clock Club: One more and I'm outta here."

The shed is a small facility that housed the lawn mowers, cutting instruments, and equipment they used to take care of the fields. The Five O'clock Club also stashed a couple coolers of beer. We'd hang out there after practice, knock down a few cold ones and enjoy the camaraderie and enlightening conversation—oh, we solved all of the world's problems in that little shed.

John Riggins cured me of wanting a regular membership in the Five O'clock Club.

One day, Riggo brought some "white lightning" that he got from one of his buddies out in the sticks. He proceeded to make sure that all of us partook. Riggo insisted: we *had* to have some.

I was a bit of a loner, so I'd usually stop, have a couple quick ones, and go.

But it started raining that day, and I decided to wait until it cleared up. Riggo wasn't going to let this opportunity pass.

"May Day, if you're gonna stay in this fucking shed and be part of the Five O'clock Club," he said, "You're drinking this shit."

"I just drink beer," I told him. "I don't drink hard liquor."

His response: "Drink it or get out!"

I drank some and passed it on. It was a long time before it came back to me.

Hog barbecues meant Hog-sized portions and comparable drinks to wash them down. Clockwise from bottom left: me, Raleigh McKenzie, George Starke (holding the bottle of bubbly), Joe Jacoby, and Joe Bugel (checking the vintage).

"Again!" Riggo insisted.

Thirty or 45 minutes later, after a few more samples, I took my first step out of the shed. You have to understand—the shed wasn't handicap accessible. There was about an 18-foot drop to the ground. I fell face first, right in the mud.

May Day was a Five O'clock Club member *in absentia* for a while.

MORE TALES OF CARLISLE

The town of Carlisle is probably best known for Carlisle College—the former Carlisle Industrial School for Indians, where the legendary Jim Thorpe began his athletic career. For more than 40 years, though, the Washington Redskins' preseason training headquarters were at nearby Dickinson College.

Unlike the fictional all-girls school in *Animal House*, Emily Dickinson College, the school in Carlisle is named for John Dickinson, a Pennsylvania governor during the Colonial period. An *Animal House* comparison is appropriate, though, since the Hogs often behaved like the boys of Delta House.

There was this bar in Carlisle called "The Fireside," which we frequented after practice during training camp, particularly the offensive linemen. It was about a two-minute drive from the practice field. You went under the train trestle, down the road, and around the corner. It had the coldest beers in town and frosted mugs.

We used to go there after every practice and hang out there until we went to our meetings.

The Fireside had a no-swearing policy. One day George Starke was telling a story about what Joe Gibbs said about a player—that "he's a tough sucker."

The guy behind the bar said, "Hey, watch that! No swearing in this place!"

"I'm just telling a story," George said. "I didn't swear. All I said was 'tough sucker.'"

"I told you to watch your swearing," He said.

"I didn't swear," George said. "I said 'tough sucker.'"

"Tough sucker?" The bartender said. "You're outta here!" and he tossed George out of the bar.

◆ ◆ ◆

If you listen to the various Hogs, it may seem like we partied a lot and drank a lot at training camp.

Well, we did.

It was always hot in Carlisle, 95 or 96 degrees and humid. Nobody wanted to practice. We'd lose eight or ten pounds at practice. We went out afterwards to have a couple of beers and relax before we went to our meetings. After all, we had to replenish the fluids and carbohydrates that we lost in that sweltering heat.

One Wednesday, we had evening practice, so we decided that, instead of going to the cafeteria for lunch, we'd go to one of the local establishments in downtown Carlisle. That day the bar had a special on hot dogs and buckets of mini-beers, those seven-ounce miniatures.

At first, we decided to have a hot dog or two and one bucket of mini-beers that Grimm, Jacoby, Bostic, and I would share. One bucket turned into two—two turned into three. One hot dog turned into four or five for some of the guys.

It was steamy and hot that evening—we just wanted to get out of there, but Coach Gibbs decided to hold the offense after practice. Joe got in the huddle, sniffed around, and smelled the alcohol. He grabbed Joe Bugel by the collar and said, "I don't know what those guys are doing, but you'd better solve this problem, and you'd better get a handle on these guys, because right now that huddle smells like garbage."

Buges started screaming at us in the huddle. Before we went to the next play, Russ barfed—right in the huddle—a grimy barf with big chunks of hot dog in it. He looked around at everybody as we turned our heads, saying "Oh my God, Russ. That's disgusting."

Undaunted by our disgust, Russ picked up a chunk of hot dog from the vomit and threw it in his mouth.

"Mmm … tasty," he said, and then swallowed it.

After practice, Bugel ran us until we dropped.

◆ ◆ ◆

During one camp, when Jim Hanifan was our offensive line coach, Grimm, Jacoby, Bostic, Raleigh McKenzie, me and the rest of the boys decided to go out after practice.

We weren't happy with the way we were being treated. We weren't playing very well during the preseason, and the coaches were being tough on us. Russ and Jake decided to revolt. They held Raleigh McKenzie hostage. They wouldn't let Raleigh leave the bar and return to practice.

"I'm not going to do this," I told them.

"Well, you go back and tell them what's going on," they said. "We're going to do this as a unit. We're doing this as a group."

I went and explained the situation to Hanifan. He started running around, sweating, saying, "You'd better get those guys back here, Footsie."

"I can't get them back here," I said. "They've drawn a line in the sand. They're staying at The Fireside."

Hanifan told Gibbs, who came running to me, asking why I couldn't get the guys back.

"I don't know; I don't control them," I said. "They're taking a position that you're being too tough on them. They're sticking together as a unit. This is it. They're digging their heals in."

The guys didn't come back for the meetings, but they came back for bed check that night.

Gibbs let them in, warning them, but they weren't fined, suspended—nothing! Instead, they were yelled at like a bunch of little kids who were caught skipping school.

Bottom line: Hanifan gave us a speech. He told us he was supposed to yell and scream at us. Instead, he was proud of us for sticking to our guns and sticking together.

Later, I got chastised for not sticking with the rest of the group.

◆　◆　◆

It seemed as if we were yelled at or lectured to on a regular basis at camp. Every year the league would give us its annual drug talk and gun policy discussion. Some guy from NFL security would come down and lecture us about the dangers of drugs and firearms. It was the exact speech, same language every year:

"If you get caught with firearms, if you get caught with drugs, your ass is grass, and *we* will be the lawn mower. If you have a gun in your room, it better not be there by tomorrow morning. If you have a gun in your car, it better be gone."

He'd also give us tips on guns at home:

"If someone breaks in your house, you are protecting your family, and you're covered. But if that person should fall out the window or the front door, make sure that you drag his ass back into your house. The legal repercussions are ten times worse if you shoot him outside your house instead of inside your house."

You have to love the NFL—always looking after our best interests.

BREAKING CAMP

Leaving Carlisle was like the Indy 500—"Gentlemen, start your engines!"

The last day of camp turned into a race down the mountains of eastern Pennsylvania to see who could get to Washington first.

It was a bet between all the players. Guys were going well over 100 miles an hour on two-lane highway roads out of Carlisle, down Route 15 to Hagerstown and then along the back way through Leesburg to get to Washington.

It was amazing, one of the biggest caravans you've ever seen—guys driving Suburbans, Mercedes, or sports cars—passing one another, weaving around one another on mountain roads. It was probably the most reckless thing most of us had ever done, but it was a challenge every year to see who could get back the fastest.

I was stopped just twice in my ten years going to and coming back from Carlisle—once going up and once coming back. Both times, I was able to negotiate myself out of the ticket.

It's good to be a Redskin.

CASINO IN THE SKY

I have to chuckle when I read about various communities debating over the merits of riverboat gambling versus a land-based casino. During my years with the Washington Redskins, there was no need for that debate. We had a "Casino in the Sky."

When you walked through our team plane to and from road games—especially after a road win—you would have thought you had just stepped into a flying gambling house.

Every type of gambling you could imagine—blackjack, dice, poker, Texas hold'em, backgammon, cribbage, gin rummy—everything.

All we needed was Robert De Niro, Sharon Stone, and a camera, and we could have made the movie. Forget about *Tilt*, the *World Series of Poker*, *Celebrity Poker Showdown*, or any of the gambling-related shows you see on television now.

We had a live reality show years before you ever heard the term.

I'd estimate half the team participated in some type of gambling on the plane, including a few of the coaches. Players wouldn't just bet on backgammon; they'd put wagers on each roll of the dice.

On one Super Bowl trip, I won a few beans playing gin rummy with Rich Caster, the tight end we picked up from the Jets. (Now, I like to think I'm a skilled gin player but, I have to admit, I ran into a good run of cards against Rich on that trip.)

The Casino in the Sky. Today's high-stakes poker programs have nothing on our team flights. Clockwise from bottom left: Greg Williams (with cigar), me, Clint Didier (ball cap), Curtis Jordan, and an unidentified dealer.

The card games continued at the hotel. Forget about going out. Why do that, when it was more fun to stay and gamble at the hotel? That may be one reason the coaches looked the other way—we couldn't get into *that* much trouble as long as we stayed at the hotel.

SUPER BOWL TICKETS

Vikings head coach Mike Tice had to be asking, "Why me?" as the NFL slapped him with a $100,000 fine for scalping Super Bowl tickets.

Vikings running back coach Dean Dalton and special teams coach Rusty Tillman were each socked with $10,000 fines for violating an NFL rule that prohibits the sale of Super Bowl tickets at more than face value.

The Vikings coaches were guilty, but the practice of scalping Super Bowl tickets has existed throughout the NFL for decades. When the Tice accusations first came to light, NFL commissioner Paul Tagliabue admitted that the resale of Super Bowl tickets was a league-wide problem, but claimed, "No other teams were found in violation."

Tice and his assistants were wrong, in clear violation of NFL rules. But they were also victims of bad timing—a time when the NFL finally decided to send a strong message about scalping Super Bowl tickets. Typical of any business or industry, the Vikings' coaches became the league scapegoats for something that had been widely accepted for years.

I can guarantee you that ticket scalping has existed league-wide for many years.

When I played with the Washington Redskins, it was standard procedure. Players and coaches sold their Super Bowl tickets—to brokers, to travel agents, to anybody who wanted to buy them.

Getting Super Bowl tickets was like hitting the lottery for members of the Redskins organization, and not for just the players and coaches. Management, public relations, equipment managers, and trainers sold their Super Bowl tickets. Some made enough for a down payment on their first homes.

Every player and assistant coach in the NFL has the right to purchase up to two Super Bowl tickets at face value. Head coaches can buy up to 12 tickets. Buyers are required to sign a form that says they won't resell them for a profit.

Jimmy Speros was an assistant weight coach for the Redskins in the early to mid-'80s. He had a contact through a travel agent who would pay big money for Super Bowl tickets. In our Super Bowl years, he would sit in the corner of the locker room and offer a certain dollar amount over the face value of the ticket.

The years we went to the Super Bowl, they gave us six tickets with the option to buy 20 or more; so you'd go to this office upstairs, buy as many as you could, write a check, and sign the form.

Then you'd walk your tickets downstairs to the corner of the locker room where Jimmy was sitting with a briefcase full of hundred-dollar bills. He'd pay you four to five times over face value for your Super Bowl tickets—*cash.*

Jimmy Speros later became the owner of the Baltimore Stallions during their brief time in the Canadian Football League. I always wondered how much money Jimmy earned toward the purchase of the Stallions with his brokering of Super Bowl tickets.

After selling Super Bowl tickets, one of our players had his money stolen from his locker. There was nothing he could do. He couldn't report it. What would he say if they asked why he had a few thousand dollars in his locker?

"Oh, I just scalped my Super Bowl tickets."

THE PERKS

Super Bowl tickets were one of the many perks we received as Washington Redskins. One thing about Jack Kent Cooke and the Washington Redskins, whatever you needed to win, you would get. The Redskins organization would always take care of its players.

This was in a time when maybe a handful of teams across the league really took care of their own, even in retirement. The Pittsburgh Steelers and the Oakland Raiders did it. The Redskins started following those examples.

The Friday following a victory, the team would treat us to a big barbecue. In addition to a great meal, it was another chance to relax and shoot the breeze together, just another way to build that team unity. They really took care of us when we won. In addition to the barbecues, we received gifts from the "Redskin community," which the team funneled to us, including lounge chairs, TVs, mini-TVs, and cash.

LEATHER BALLS

You don't realize how much a guy can be motivated by a little bit of incentive. The Redskins "community" donated all kinds of items that the team used as rewards or incentives—colored TVs, hand-held TVs, lounge chairs, all kinds of things. It wasn't necessarily the gift. It was a tremendous feeling to stand before your teammates and receive a memento for an outstanding performance, either individually or as part of a unit like the Hogs. Guys were motivated by it; it gave a sense of pride.

One year the coaches decided they just wanted a bunch of "tough suckers" on the team. If the coaches deemed you "tough enough" that week, you got the "Leather Ball Award."

For a week, you got a parking spot right up front. And best of all, you got to keep the Leather Balls Award. It was nothing more than tiny balls in a leather pouch on a leather string. You wouldn't believe how our players—grown men—longed for the Leather Balls Award.

I'm proud to say I was a recipient of the Leather Balls Award. I hung mine on the rear-view mirror of my SUV. They stayed there for about four years.

HOG WILD

As members of the Hogs, we were always getting pig-related gifts, including all kinds of pork products. Apparently, one guy didn't think our edible gift packages were fresh enough, because he offered every one of us a live piglet.

Most of the guys didn't want to be bothered, but I made a couple phone calls and worked out a deal with a local farmer. I gave him three of the piglets, and he agreed to raise one for me. Once he got fat enough, I hosted the Washington Redskins' Hawaiian Shirt Hog Party and Pig Roast.

My fellow porcine cohorts, the ones who couldn't be bothered with their piglet, sucked down plenty of ribs in short order.

THE FANS

Keith Jackson delivered one of the best lines I've ever heard following a particularly flowery introduction as a luncheon speaker. Keith's response went something like this: "Thank you for that wonderful introduction, but just as my granddaddy used to say, 'If you can't eat it, drink it, cash it, smoke it, or sleep with it, it ain't worth a darn thing.'"

I love the line even if some of the benefits I received as a Washington Redskin don't fit into any of those categories. One of the most remarkable, intangible gifts we enjoyed as Redskins was the tremendous support and love we received from the incredible fans. There are some great football fans throughout the country, but I don't think the fans in any other city compare to those in Washington.

When we won Super Bowls—even when we lost in Super Bowl XVIII—hundreds of thousands of fans lined the streets for our homecoming parades. Prior to our first Super Bowl

I've always enjoyed cooking (almost as much as eating). During one off-season I wrote *Mark May's Hog Cookbook*, a selection of simple, but tasty recipes for Hog-sized appetites. The book is in the David Walker Lupton African American Cookbook Collection at the University of Alabama (and on sale at my website).

parade—after winning Super Bowl XVIII—I had never experienced such a mass outpouring of emotion.

The weather turned nasty on the morning of the parade and never got better—a cold, driving rain. It was impossible to reschedule. During the bus ride from Redskin Park in suburban Virginia, we all talked about how the rain would wash out the celebration, but we'd be good sports and go through the motions.

Shortly after crossing the Potomac River, we couldn't believe our eyes. The Redskin fans were out in full force, 500,000 strong. People were EVERYWHERE, on tops of buildings, light poles, and street signs. Banners hung from office buildings and federal buildings throughout the downtown area. In some ways, it was a bigger high than winning the game itself. Big bad football players, the world champions, were tearing up.

Originally we were scheduled to ride in convertibles along the parade route, but due to the rain we stayed in the team buses. We reached out the windows to shake hands with the fans. I wouldn't be surprised if a cold brew or two passed through the open windows.

The fans barely noticed John Riggins's absence. Riggo overslept and missed the parade.

The fans in Washington were always enthusiastic, but I felt the intensity escalate during the 1982 playoffs. We beat the Detroit Lions and Minnesota Vikings in the first two rounds. Near the end of the Vikings game, once we had locked up the victory, the fans turned RFK Stadium into one big party room.

They jumped up and down, chanting, "WE WANT DALLAS! WE WANT DALLAS!"

Had we not already taken control of the game, the Vikings might have packed it in right then and there. On one side of the stadium, there's a gap—two to three feet—between the bottom of the stands and the stadium floor. As the fans stomped up and down, the bottom of the stands—a whole section of the stadium—repeatedly slapped the field. POW! POW! POW! I thought the whole side of the stadium was going to collapse.

One by one, the Viking linemen nudged each other and pointed to that spectacle. They were completely intimidated.

After the game, a friend of mine asked if I saw what happened. I remember saying, "Oh yeah. I saw, and so did the Vikings. I'm just glad that I'm on this side."

Riggo rushed 37 times for 185 yards against the Vikings that day. He also left the game in style. With about a minute to go, Joe Gibbs pulled Riggo out of the game so the fans could show their appreciation. With the place going bonkers, Riggo stopped at midfield, pulled off his helmet, put his hand across his waist, and then bowed to both sides of the stadium.

◆　◆　◆

I didn't think it possible, but our fans were cranked even more for Dallas the next week. We lost only one game during the 1982 season, 24-10 at Dallas in early December. We had the home-field advantage since the Cowboys lost twice during the regular season. Some of our critics believed that Dallas was the better team; that Washington was a fluke in the strike-shortened season. The NFC Championship game at RFK Stadium was our chance for revenge and retribution.

Our fans hated the Cowboys as much as we did, some even more. The atmosphere was indescribable. Both emotionally and physically, it was one of the greatest games that I've ever played and certainly one of the most satisfying victories of my entire football career.

We didn't exactly kick their butts from start to finish. It was a typical Redskin-Cowboy dogfight in the trenches with the usual assortment of fights and arguments. We did dominate at crunch time and beat the Cowboys, 31-17.

Now I'd like to think we would've won the rematch on any field, in any stadium—but I will never discount the emotional lift provided by the Washington Redskin faithful at RFK.

◆   ◆   ◆

I loved interacting with our fans after a game. After you showered, after you met with the media, after you got dressed and, if necessary, got treatment, the fans were still outside to greet you—thousands of them.

I felt like a rock star walking through the parking lot with fans shaking my hand, asking for my autograph, handing me some food or a cold drink, or just reaching out to touch me. They'd invite us to their tailgate parties, even after a loss.

Fortunately, I had family and friends to help me keep it all in perspective, at least most of the time. Every now and then, I'd get a little wake-up call from an outside source.

◆   ◆   ◆

During one game at RFK, I twisted or turned an ankle. It wasn't serious, but the trainers put me on crutches after the game, just to keep the weight off my ankle (when you're a Hog, the weight factor is huge).

After leaving the locker room, I followed my usual path to my car and made my way through the cheering Redskins fans, a little slower than usual. I knew my friends had an ice-cold beer waiting for me. I could almost taste it. As much I enjoy mingling with the fans, I wanted to extricate myself from the adoring throng quickly but politely.

A man with his young son, who was probably eight or nine years old, approached me. I have a special soft spot for kids. I always try to spend a little extra time with them. This one was something special. The little boy was in a wheelchair. I'm not sure what confined him to the wheelchair, nor did I ask—but it appeared it was not a short-term deal.

He looked up at me with a huge grin, and with his two little arms, he held out a pen and a piece of scrap paper for an autograph. Suddenly the smile on his face turned to a look of concern, even fear. The fact that I was on crutches had just dawned on him.

With his bottom lip quivering, he asked me in his tiny voice, "Are you going to be okay, Mr. May?"

This little guy was in a wheelchair, *and he was worried about me!*

I assured him that I would fine. I joked with him, and we talked for a while about football and where he went to school and any number of subjects. After a while, a small crowd had gathered around us. Mind you, these were Redskin fans who wanted to talk about the game or wanted an autograph for themselves, but everyone was cool. Nobody interrupted. They just watched and listened to us—it was a wonderful moment.

Finally, the dad said something like, "Come on, son. We've taken up enough of his time."

Again, my new little buddy held out the paper and pen and asked, "Mr. May, would you mind signing this for me?"

I immediately thought, "Certainly I can do better than this piece of scrap paper. If I only had a helmet, or jersey or football."

As if reading my thoughts, one of the fans offered his game program and said, "Mark, would you rather sign this for him?" What a wonderful gesture.

As the boy and father turned to leave, the father looked at me and mouthed a silent but very sincere, "Thank you."

All I could think was, "No sir, I should be thanking you."

Perspective.

◆ ◆ ◆

Thanks to the Washington Redskins, I was able to travel with a couple USO tours through the National Football League and U.S. Department of Defense. I went once to the Pacific Rim and once to Europe.

Russ Francis, the tight end from the 49ers, was along for the European tour. It's a shame Russ was born before the X-Games became popular. Russ was into flying, parachuting, parasailing—"Mr. Thrill Seeker."

While in Germany, we took our rented mini-Mercedes bus for a little drive along the Autobahn. We were tooling along at about 125 miles per hour—fast enough for me but not quite adventurous enough for Mr. Francis. He decided it would be "cool" to sit on top of the bus. He crawled atop and thought that was the greatest thing in the world.

I was scared shitless, plus I could see the headline: "Helpless Mark May Watches Russ Francis Fall to His Death." Finally, I'd had enough; I grabbed him by the legs and dragged his butt back into the van.

Russ sat there giggling, saying, "That was cool, man. I'm gonna do it again."

I just looked at him and said, "It ain't gonna happen, dude."

San Francisco tight end Russ Francis (right) was a real "trip" on one of my NFL-USO trips. I was able to keep Russ inside the vehicle most of the time.

DIEGO GARCIA AND HECTOR THE HAMMERHEAD

When I first heard our USO tour was traveling to the island of Diego Garcia, I figured we were headed somewhere off the coast of Spain or South America. I would have flunked geography test.

Diego Garcia is a small (17 square miles) horseshoe-shaped island a few degrees south of the equator in the middle of the Indian Ocean—an area known as the British Indian Ocean Territory (BIOT). Diego Garcia is owned by Great Britain, but the United States has a lease there. Both countries have military bases on the island.

We flew to Diego Garcia from the Philippines aboard a military transport plane. The pilots, of course, were up front. We were crammed in eight seats in the back of the plane behind all the military equipment.

When we took off from the Philippines, it was about 105 degrees, so we were all in shorts and T-shirts. About 30 minutes later, we were flying at an altitude of about 25,000 feet—freezing our butts off and fighting over blankets. The flight lasted seven or eight hours. Next to my draft-day excursion in 1981 from Pittsburgh to Washington, this was my flight from hell.

Once we got close enough to descend and warm up, everything was great. The water around Diego Garcia is probably the most beautiful I've ever seen. It is crystal clear. I would swear you could look down in the water and see for 200 yards.

The fishing was magnificent but came with a warning from our guides: "Do not go into the water."

"Sure," we thought. "You're trying to scare the big, bad football players from America."

Our guides repeated, "Do NOT go in the water."

We looked down and saw some sharks, but they weren't very big.

Our military hosts then told us the story of Hector the Hammerhead, the Jaws of Diego Garcia. Several years earlier, a local fisherman had reeled in a six-foot tiger shark. According to the tale, a hammerhead shark, nearly 30 feet in length, then breached onto the back of the boat, bit off three-fourths of the tiger shark, and disappeared into the deep.

We just *knew* this was one big fish story.

When we returned to the base, they showed us pictures of the legendary Hector. His mouth was about six feet across and, yes … there was a tiger shark in his mouth.

Since Hector's demise, there had been reported sightings of a Hector II. I didn't know if that was fact or fiction, but I was in no particular hurry to find out. From that point on, we heeded every word of advice, especially, "Don't go in the water."

I was still in my shirt sleeves as we got ready to take off from the Philippines during another USO tour. By the time we reached altitude, I was huddled in a blanket, freezing my little derriere off (okay, my big derriere).

I'm just thankful Russ Francis wasn't along for the Diego Garcia trip. That nut job would have swam or windsurfed in that water.

◆   ◆   ◆

On my Pacific Rim trip, I also got to see the Philippines, Tokyo, and Korea. One of the fascinating portions of that trip was the time I spent in the Demilitarized Zone (DMZ) in Korea.

Certain visitors or dignitaries, such as our group, were allowed to go inside the meeting room where all the negotiations have taken place. A line in the middle of the room represents the 38th parallel, which splits the two Koreas. We were permitted to walk around the negotiating table, technically into North Korea, when we stepped over that line. Wanting to leave my mark in Communist Korea, I reached into my pocket and pulled out a Washington Redskins sticker. As I walked around the table, I stuck the little decal underneath the table on the North Korean side. I didn't tell anyone until we were on the buses heading back to our hotel in Seoul.

About three hours later, I got a call in my room. It was Bill Granholm, the NFL's liaison for the trip. Bill is a great guy, very fun, but then he sounded very stern.

"Mark, you have to pack everything you have and be down in the lobby in ten minutes," he demanded.

"What are you talking about?" I asked.

"Mark, I'm not going to say it again. You have ten minutes to pack all your belongings and be down in the lobby."

So I packed my suitcase and headed for the lobby, wondering what was happening. Are they kicking us out? Have the Communists invaded South Korea? Is there some impending natural disaster?

When I got to the lobby, I saw Bill standing there with an MP.

"Okay," I said, "What the hell is happening?"

"Mark, did you put a sticker under the table on the North Korean side?" Bill asked.

"Yes," I said. "What's the big deal?"

"That is an international incident," Bill told me. "That's the big deal. You have to leave the country immediately. No appeal. No discussion. It's a government decision. You must go *now*."

I looked at the MP and said, "He's kidding, isn't he?"

He was like the Queen's Guard—no words, no expression.

"Aw, shit. What have I done?" I thought. I started to wonder if I *could* get out of the country. I started to think about

ABOVE: Among my most rewarding experiences as a pro football player were my trips to U.S. military bases with the NFL-USO tours. Here I'm talking with a solider in the South Korean territory of Panmunjom, along the Demilitarized Zone (DMZ) between North and South Korea.

BELOW: I can't add much to that slogan—it makes "Win One for the Gipper" seem a little puny. If I ever use military terms in reference to football—war, battle, etc.—they are meant strictly within the context of the game. Our men and women in the armed services are the ones who put it on the line for us.

ABOVE: A U.S. MP and South Korean soldier posted near the DMZ.

BELOW: Our NFL-USO tour group inside the meeting room in the DMZ. That microphone cord along the table is the dividing line between North and South Korea. I left a little "souvenir" under the table on the North Korean side.

Our entire group for the NFL-USO tour in the Pacific Rim. From left to right: military escort, Greg Bingham (Houston Oilers), Mike Davis (Raiders), military escort, Ray Wersching (Raiders), Linden King (Raiders), Bill Granholm (NFL escort), me, and military escort.

all the stories I had read about American civilians in foreign prisons. Scenes from *Midnight Express* flashed through my mind.

We got about three yards from the door, and all the guys I was traveling with came out from hiding, laughing their asses off. Bill just about doubled over. Even the MP started to laugh. I was looking around for Dick Clark and Ed McMahon.

Fortunately, there were no video cameras to capture that practical joke for posterity. But ABC got wind of the story while televising the Seoul Olympics the next year. The network sent a camera crew to the DMZ and, sure enough, the sticker was still there.

JUST FAKING IT

I'm sure we'll see the NFL start to crack down more on ticket scalping following the Mike Tice "scandal." The league has already tightened up its rules governing players' injuries.

While playing for the Redskins, I became close with Bobby Beathard, Charlie Casserly, Billy Devaney, and Dickie Daniels. They were great guys and probably the best in the business at what they did.

Before the NFL looked closer at the injury rules, every team tried to horde players. I believe the Redskins were the masters at it.

We basically had a practice team—guys who would come up with a variety of twinges or pulls and end up on injured reserve. Although they had potential, they probably wouldn't contribute *that* season. You didn't want to waste a roster spot, but you didn't want to let them go, either. So players would come up with mysterious injuries and be placed on the injured list.

Many of these players would practice against the players on the roster. Think of that—they were on injured reserve but practiced. It was also a way to groom those players into your system.

THE INJURY

When I went down with a knee injury in '89, I wasn't faking what kept me off the playing field for a year and a half.

I had been fortunate to that point. Sure, I experienced the normal aches and pains associated with life in the National Football League—bumps, bruises, sprains, pulls, broken noses, even a broken bone or two. But I had managed to escape serious injury through more than eight NFL seasons.

My good fortune ended in week nine of the 1989 season, a home game against the Dallas Cowboys (wouldn't you know!). It was a broken play. Raleigh McKenzie tripped over Jeff Bostic and into me.

I never saw it coming, but I heard it. It sounded like a shotgun blast: *Bam!* Instant pain.

I rolled over on it, and when I did, my leg was bent out—with my brace. I rolled back over, and it popped back in.

Team doctor Charlie Jackson and trainer Bubba Tyer rushed onto the field. Charlie touched my knee and said, "It doesn't look good. We'll call the stretcher."

I wasn't having that.

"No way! You're not carting me off the field!" I said. "I'll limp or you can hold me up. I am NOT getting carted off!"

They realized it was useless to argue. They probably also wanted to get my butt off the field as quickly as possible.

When we got to the sidelines, I said, "It doesn't feel that bad. Why don't you test it again?

Charlie said, "Mark, trust me. It's gone." He did a flexibility test on my knee. He popped it out to the left about three inches, put it back, and said, "No."

When we went back to the locker room, everybody seemed more upset than I was. Not that it was my brightest moment, but I figured if I had gone that long without a major injury, I was due.

The weird thing was that my knee never really swelled. I never really swelled with any injury I had. I'd go to the trainer and say, "This is really bothering me."

"No, no," they'd say. "Don't worry about it. You'll be fine."

The only time I ever swelled was after I had that surgery. I think my body decided to make up for all the times I didn't swell. But the surgeons had to do a lot of "tinkering" to get the job done.

They had to break the top of my bone and take out a third of the patella tendon. Then they grafted my patella tendon with two screws where my ACL should have been. It was totally gone, and they put a staple in my knee where my media collateral was gone. That wasn't much fun.

Just two weeks before the knee injury, I had broken my wrist in the first quarter against the Buccaneers. I banged it on some guy's helmet.

The doctor and trainers looked at it, didn't see any swelling, and said, "Nah, don't worry about it. We'll put some tape on it."

I went to them again at halftime.

"Man, this is really bothering me," I said.

They told me, "You have a pretty bad bruise, but you'll be fine."

After the game, they X-rayed the wrist. I took a shower, got dressed, and was ready to leave when Bubba called me over.

"May Day, we need to see you," he said.

He put the X-rays up—he and Charlie Jackson—and gave me the news: "You broke your wrist, and this bone chipped off, and it's about the size of a nickel. We'll have to put you in a cast."

ASTAPHAN

During my rehabilitation period, I took a vacation to the Jack Tar Village resort on the Caribbean island of St. Kitts. I was at the casino, limping from table to table as this guy walked up to me.

He told me he was a doctor and asked me if I was an athlete.

I explained that I was a pro football player who had sustained an ACL injury, and I was looking forward to a long and difficult rehab period.

He told me he could get me back on the playing field in less than two months. This guy was smooth. I don't know about ice to an Eskimo, but he could peddle sand to a Caribbean beachcomber.

I was tempted to take him up on his offer. When you're an injured professional athlete, you'll *consider* just about anything to get back in action. I told him I'd have to think about it. He gave me his card.

When I got back to the States, I told a friend about the encounter in St. Kitts. He asked me for the guy's name.

I didn't have his card on me, but I managed, "A Dr. Jamie *something. ...*"

This friend, a big track and field enthusiast, started laughing and said, "It wasn't Jamie Astaphan, was it?"

I couldn't believe it. "How the hell did you know that?"

"Damn, May Day," he said. "You have a doctor named Jamie, who claims to work miracles for athletes and lives on St. Kitts. Who else could it be but Jamie Astaphan? He was Ben Johnson's doctor."

Then it hit me. Dr. George "Jamie" Astaphan was the physician who supplied steroids to Ben Johnson, the Canadian sprinter who won the 100-meter dash at the 1988 Olympics Games. After testing positive at the Games, he was stripped of his gold medal and banned from the sport.

Astaphan was never charged with a crime in the Ben Johnson case, but later he was convicted in Florida for conspiracy to distribute steroids and cocaine. The last I heard he had returned to St. Kitts to practice medicine.

HILARITY OPEN

One of the most anticipated Redskin outings every year was the Hilarity Open, a charity golf tournament put together by our trainers, headed by Keoke Kamau. We all got dressed up in the wildest suits we could assemble: purple shirts, pink panties, bikinis, wild hats.

We played at the local golf course in Herndon. All the money went to charity. We probably raised several thousand dollars for a local charity and had a blast.

All the guys really let down their hair. You have to understand that the Washington Redskins weren't all a bunch of Hogs or the Fun Bunch. We also had some very conservative players on the team. But their sartorial inhibitions disappeared at the Hilarity Open.

If you had been at the Hilarity Open, you would have seen some of the most respected and conservative members of the Redskins organization dressed in short shorts or bikinis, halter tops, or polka-dot shirts and hats. Even some of our stuffed shirts got a little crazy at the Hilarity Open.

Even the most conservative Washington Redskins (yes, there were a few) let their hair down at the annual Hilarity Open Charity Golf Classic.

CHARLIE TEN HITCH

My father got me hooked on harness racing. He took me to Vernon Downs and Monticello Raceway in Saratoga when I was a kid. We used to go in the summer all the time. I loved it and decided then I would go into the horse-racing business.

When I was at the University of Pittsburgh, I met with harness racing great Del Miller at the Meadows raceway outside of Pittsburgh. Del took me under his wing. He taught me the insides of the horse business. That served to whet my appetite even more.

Once I became a professional football player, I was able to purchase some horses. I fell into a great one, which I bought as a two-year-old in training. I decided to name my yearlings and babies after Redskins' plays. This one I named, "Charlie Ten Hitch," after one of our play action passes.

My father instilled in me a great love of harness racing at an early age. Fortunately, the horses I owned usually got to pull a much lighter load.

On the field, the Charlie Ten Hitch was one of our bread-and-butter plays. On the track, Charlie Ten Hitch was my biggest breadwinner. I found a wonderful trainer named Donna Williams. In 1990 Charlie won the Peter Haughton Memorial Trot at the Meadowlands. The Peter Haughton is like the Super Bowl for two-year-old trotters. That year the total purse was $609,250.

It was an incredible race. Charlie broke at the start, made up 15 lengths and then held off "Super Pleasure," a 4-5 favorite. I was sole owner of Charlie. His win represented the biggest stakes win ever for a sole African-American owner.

As a two-year-old, Charlie Ten Hitch lost only one race and won $366,499—not bad for an initial $20,000 investment. Of all my professional ventures—pro football, automobile dealerships, sportscasting—Charlie Ten Hitch brought me the most pride as a businessman.

The best part of the whole experience was having my father with me in the winner's circle at the Meadowlands. He was the person who sparked my interest in the horse-racing industry. To share that moment was an unbelievable experience.

That was the year I was rehabbing my knee. I was already in the car business, and my horse performed like an All-Pro. I made more money from the horse than I did from football that year.

Joe Gibbs, Bobby Beathard, and Charlie Casserly thought for sure I'd hang up my cleats.

"Hell, no," I told them. "I'm not retiring."

ROCKET SCREEN RIGHT

Whenever I tell people I named my horses after Redskins plays, they'll usually ask me if I named one after *the* play in Super Bowl XVIII against the Raiders. We called it "Rocket

Screen Right," and though successful overall, it is probably the most infamous play call in Redskins history.

We were already trailing the Raiders, 14-3, and had the ball on our own 12-yard line with a few seconds left in the first half. Joe Gibbs called for the "Rocket Screen Right," a screen pass from Joe Theismann to Joe Washington—at least that was the plan.

We had used the play a couple times during the regular season for big games, but the Raiders saw it coming. Their linebackers were yelling, "Watch for the screen!" but Theismann never heard them. Raider linebacker Jack Squirek intercepted and took it in for a touchdown. Instead of trailing by 11 points at halftime, we were down 18. Our momentum was shot. We ended up losing, 38-9.

Despite that huge misstep with the play, the "Rocket Screen" was very successful for us overall. Considering that, and not wanting to seem like the superstitious type, I named one of my yearlings Rocket Screen Right.

The rat never made it to the track. He made it to the training track but was never good enough to make it to the racetrack. That was probably for the better. I would have hated to see him lose to some nag named "Squirek's Luck."

I think he's still pulling a cart up in Amish country right now.

MY PRO BOWL

The best bet I ever lost involved my selection to the Pro Bowl following the 1988 season. By that time in my career, I had given up serious consideration of making the Pro Bowl. We had so many of the Hogs make it already—Russ Grimm, Joe Jacoby, Jeff Bostic, R.C. Theilmann, Jim Lachey—I didn't think

I had a chance. I even made reservations for a Caribbean vacation during Pro Bowl week.

Since the players selected Pro Bowlers, my reputation as a dirty player probably didn't help my cause. I don't know how much of a factor that was, but several teammates believed that. Charles Mann, our Pro Bowl defensive tackle, stated so publicly. If that's the case, I can live with it—that's the path I chose.

At the time, I was seriously dating Kathy Feldick, a pretty blonde from Iowa. On more than one occasion, Kathy "hinted" that she was ready for a permanent relationship. Finally I said, "We'll get married when I make the Pro Bowl."

Imagine my surprise when I learned that I was selected to play in the Pro Bowl game in Honolulu. If I didn't know better, I'd say the players in the NFC heard about my promise and voted for me as their way of getting me back.

If that's the case, I still got in the final shot. I kept my word. Kathy and I were married during Pro Bowl week in Hawaii. We remain happily married and have two beautiful daughters—Abra and Bryce.

MIKE DITKA

As a member of the 1989 NFC Pro Bowl team, I fully expected Mike Ditka, head coach for the NFC, to be his usual hard-ass self. But Ditka was cool—real cool.

At our first team meeting, he told us, "We're not going out in pads. We're gonna be on the practice field for 45 minutes, no more. We're gonna play some golf. We're gonna have fun. And, we're gonna win the damn game, because the winner's share is more than the loser's share."

Mike was true to his word. We practiced for about 45 minutes—tops. Everything was a walk-through. We went through a couple drills, had a short team period, and then got the hell off the field. We were back on the beach or playing golf by noon.

Marv Levy had his AFC Pro Bowlers out in full pads for 90 minutes or more. We were out of the showers and headed back to the hotel as they were just leaving the field.

As a fellow alumnus of the University of Pittsburgh, I've known Mike Ditka for many years, but his low-key approach to the Pro Bowl caught me off guard.

His strategy worked, though. We blasted the AFC 34-3 in one of the biggest routs in Pro Bowl history. I might have a different evaluation of "Coach" if I had played for Mike Ditka full time.

But I'll take his Pro Bowl philosophy any day.

It was great to see Mike on September 27, 2001, when the University of Pittsburgh retired my jersey at halftime of the Pitt-Miami game. Mike was one of seven Pitt players whose jersey was retired before mine, all of whom attended that night. What an incredible thrill it was for me—on the night my jersey was retired—to walk out on that field with seven of the greatest names in Pitt Panther football history: Mike Ditka, Marshall Goldberg, Joe Schmidt, Tony Dorsett, Hugh Green, Dan Marino, and Bill Fralic. All have been inducted into the College Football Hall of Fame. I was selected for the College Hall of Fame earlier this year (2005) and will be inducted next August.

In our prime years, I think the eight of us would have been a good starter set for an NFL franchise.

STRIKES AND THE UNION

The NFL players who went on strike in 1982 and 1987 suffered greatly. The NFL Players Association told us those strikes were for our betterment. Certainly, the salaries have escalated. Redskins offensive lineman Chris Samuels recently inked a $15.3 signing bonus. You could take the Hogs—all five starters—from 1981 through 1990—and their base salaries total wouldn't come close to $15.3 million. In 1985, the salaries of the five starting Hogs combined was a little more than one million dollars.

◆   ◆   ◆

The first players' strike in which I was involved—a 56-day walkout during the 1982 season—was a real eye-opener. Several teammates asked to borrow money from me to get by during the strike. I was shocked. NFL players weren't making the mega-bucks they do today, but it was still a damn good living. These guys, some who had been in the league for a few years, hadn't put anything away. They were still living week to week. Sure, I was a first-round draft pick the year before with a healthy signing bonus, but I was only a year or so out of college. I wasn't the Bank of America.

◆   ◆   ◆

During the 1987 strike, the NFL decided to bring in scabs to replace us, a situation that inspired the movie *The Replacements*. What a joke that was. It was more or less a picnic for us. The wives would bring picnic baskets and dine with us on the picket lines.

The longer I stayed in the NFL, the greater insight I got into the players' union and its heavy-handed tactics. The average lifespan for an NFL player is a little more than three years.

The NFLPA brainwashes all the rookies. The union honchos get the youngsters to sign these car contracts or endorsement contracts with companies like Reebok or Nike. They're brainwashed for the first three years. They think the union is great.

The players pay extremely high union dues. But the NFLPA is one of the weakest unions in major professional sports history. Compared to baseball, it's an atrocious joke. The pension is virtually nothing.

The union leaders, headed by Gene Upshaw, are worse than the Mafia. They run the bus over the older players. Everything is geared to the younger players. That's why you see these huge signing bonuses go to the younger players.

In four, five, or six years, players finally figure this out. One realizes his pension is terrible, and the union really isn't doing anything for him. The older you get in the NFL, the less they care about you and the less voice you have. If you look at the NFL, you don't see a vast majority of older players—the ones who have figured out the union have figured out you need better benefits, and you need a better pension.

Gene Upshaw and his thugs from the union are making six or seven figures. Upshaw is making a couple million dollars. Who approves their salaries and raises? They do!

Upshaw will sit at the head of the union and say, "I want a 15-percent raise, and you guys will get a 10-percent raise."

Like the sycophants in *Blazing Saddles*, his minions will go, "Harrumph, harrumph, harrumph, harrumph."

Gene, like Governor Le Petomane, will grab somebody and say, "I didn't get a harrumph out of you. If I don't get a harrumph, you're out of here." That's just about how they operate.

Nobody tests these people. Nobody asks Gene Upshaw, "Why don't we do this? Why do we continue to do things so you guys continue to have your cushy jobs forever?"

During one of the strikes, New Orleans kicker Russell Erxleben publicly questioned the union. He received threatening phone calls.

When players are old enough and wise enough to challenge the union, the pool of those players is diminished; there is little chance a voice will be heard. The younger players are too naïve to realize they're going to be in your shoes a few years down the road. The union has already front-loaded these guys, enticing them with the car contracts and endorsements.

Gene Upshaw and his crew have jobs for life. Their pension plan is ten times better than the players they represent. If any player looked at the union's pension plan and retirement plan, he'd take a big Eureka into the NFLPA and clean house.

Gene Upshaw is a Jesse James without a mask. That could be the title of his book: *How to Rob the NFL Players without a Gun or a Mask.*

Did you ever notice when Upshaw visits teams in Arizona or southern California, it's nearly always when the weather is bad up north—a nice paid vacation. Of course, the union meetings are held annually in Hawaii as well.

Actually, I have to commend Gene and his gang. It's a great racket—a great gig. You have a job that pays you six or seven figures, you get all your expenses, you can vote on your own raises, and nobody will question you.

They don't even have to run for office.

THE INVASION OF DALLAS

We came within two points of a perfect regular season in 1983. We lost to Dallas 31-30 in the season opener and fell one point short in week seven at Green Bay, 48-47.

We lost the "track meet" in Green Bay when Mark Moseley missed a 39-yard field goal with three seconds left. However, that didn't sting near as much the Dallas loss—when we blew a 23-3 halftime lead at home.

We got another shot at the Cowboys in the second to last week of the season. We wanted the rematch bad—*really* bad, so we came up with a little plan to demonstrate our team unity.

Taking a cue from John Riggins and Dave Butz, who often wore camouflage outfits to practice, we all went out and bought our own army fatigues, paratrooper boots, and Special Forces berets.

Normally, Joe Gibbs required us to wear nice clothes on the team flights—a coat and tie or a nice shirt with slacks. For the flight to Dallas, he allowed us to extend the dress code. The cabin of the plane was a sea of khaki and green. There was one notable exception—always his own man, Riggo forsook the combat look and dressed in civvies.

I don't know how much of an effect our sartorial splendor really produced, but we destroyed the Cowboys, 31-10. We closed out the regular season with nine straight wins, but none was as sweet as our "invasion" of Dallas.

Now, I don't where you can buy battle fatigues on a Sunday night in the D.C. area, but when we got back to Washington that night, our usual entourage of Redskin fans was there to greet us.

Many of them were dressed in camouflage outfits.

SUPER BOWL GIFTS

Joe Theismann and John Riggins were polar opposites in many respects, but both deserved and received respect on the football field. Joe and Riggo were great football players and tremendous competitors.

They also both adhered to a very wise philosophy: keep your offensive line happy. In the off-season following our victory in Super Bowl XVII, Joe and John each presented the Hogs with unique gifts to show their appreciation.

Since Riggo considered us "the strongest and most powerful offensive line in the NFL," he bought us some firepower to match. Riggo gave each of us a special edition Weatherby Mark V Deluxe hunting rifle, the most powerful shoulder-fired rifle in the world, the kind used to hunt elephants and rhinoceroses in Africa. Riggo had them engraved with our names and "Super Bowl XVII."

He also gave us one .460 Magnum cartridge each—the most powerful commercial cartridge in the world. Imagine that: we had the world's most potent weapon of its kind in the world and one bullet. We were like a combination of Ernest Hemingway, Dirty Harry, and Barney Fife—only the Mayberry deputy would've needed a larger shirt pocket. The .460 cartridge looks like a mini-missile—four or five inches long— and delivers nearly four tons of muzzle energy.

The rifles were beautiful and probably cost Riggo about $2,500 each back in 1984. But what were we going to do with them? Outside of the Republicans, I'm not familiar with any pachyderms indigenous to the Washington area.

These guns were not designed for novices. The recoil—the "kickback" when fired—is immense, even for a big, bad NFL lineman.

That didn't stop fellow Hog Ron Saul, who probably saw a few "pink elephants" during his nightly excursions with Riggo. Ron put a scope on his rifle and decided to try it out. Ron came in the next day for practice with a butterfly bandage on the bridge of his nose. The recoil was so powerful that it kicked back and popped him right behind the eyes, cutting his forehead. Naturally, Riggo was along for the experiment. He had cuts all over his hands.

I did not participate in the rifle tryout. Mine remains unused and unfired—a gunnery virgin. After spending a sufficient number of Sundays getting head-slapped by the likes of Reggie White, I had no desire to get the same treatment from a Weatherby.

Joe Theismann's gift to the Hogs was more sedate. Joe gave each Hog individual portraits—paintings of each lineman in his uniform. They are beautifully done, and I'm sure they cost Joe a pretty penny. But I thought, "What the hell am I going to do with this? Where can I hang it? In my house? How egotistical would that look?"

John and Joe probably got us the gifts that they would have enjoyed receiving. Riggo, the fullback, chose the rifle—TOO MUCH rifle.

Joe, like a typical quarterback, thought to himself, "Now, what would *I* want as a gift? Why, a portrait of *me*, of course."

Seriously, the gifts from Joe and John were very thoughtful and are cherished reminders of an extraordinary period of my life.

SUPERSTARS

I went from the Super Bowl to the Superstars in 1984. Right after the Raiders waxed us in Tampa, I returned to the Florida for the ABC *Superstars* competition.

The *Superstars* competition was a made-for-TV event created by Roone Arledge in 1973. The original idea was to bring together athletes of diverse specialties to compete in a decathlon-type competition of various sports. A host of derivative programs have followed over the years, including the *Battle of the Network Stars*, *Challenge of the Sexes*, and *Celebrity Challenge of the Sexes*. The NFL now has its own variation, but it all started in February of 1973.

Contestants that inaugural year included Rod Laver (tennis), Jean Claude Killy (alpine skiing), Johnny Unitas (football), Johnny Bench (baseball), and Joe Frazier (boxing). Olympic pole vault champion Bob Seagren, a late addition, won the inaugural *Superstars*, though many viewers best remember the initial event for Frazier's swan dive as a swimmer (Smokin' Joe nearly drowned).

Unfortunately, we didn't have footage of Boom-Boom Mancini running me ragged on the tennis court.

The year I competed, Tom Petranoff—the javelin world record holder—won the overall competition. Petranoff had a distinct advantage over the rest of us. He told me that he had trained exclusively for the *Superstars* for two months. Guys like me or Cliff Branch and Bill Pickel of the Raiders had virtually just stepped off the football field. We had to compete against a guy who had specifically trained for this competition.

I still fared pretty well. I won the weight lifting competition and placed high—second or third—in bowling.

Then I faced boxer Ray "Boom-Boom" Mancini in tennis. Ray was only about five foot two, and as a lightweight, he couldn't have weighed more than 135 pounds. In other words, May Day was nearly two Boom-Booms.

Ray was a great guy, a lot of fun to be around, but that little sucker snookered me big time during the warm-up period. I figured I could simply overpower him on the court. Sure enough, during warmups, I nailed some big serves—ace after ace. Ray just watched them go by, as if he had no chance to get a racket on one of my booming serves. I thought, "This one's in the bag."

However, once the match started, Boom-Boom lowered the boom. He ran me ragged. I thought Lawrence Taylor was quick, but Mancini was unbelievable. He got to everything and dusted my butt in about 30 minutes.

Later in the competition, I decided to take a page from Boom-Boom's book. One of the events added to the *Superstars* in its second year was the obstacle course, similar to the one Richard Gere traversed in *An Officer and a Gentleman*. And, like the course in the film, one of our obstacles was a wall. You had to grab a rope and pull yourself up as you "walked" the 12-foot barrier.

Baseball star Reggie Jackson, one of the commentators for the broadcast that year, came over to the obstacle course during one of my early run-throughs. As I got ready to practice on the wall, he watched with great interest.

"There's no way that big body is going over that wall," Reggie said.

Just as Mancini did against me in the tennis warmups, I sandbagged my practice on the wall. If you had seen me struggle on that wall, you would have thought for sure Reggie was right. He just stood there and laughed his ass off.

During the actual competition, I could just imagine what Mr. October was saying as I passed through the early stages of the obstacle course, particularly as I approached the wall.

I hit that wall and scaled it as slick as you please. When I got to the top, I turned and pointed to the broadcast booth, pumped my fist, hopped over, and continued the course. As I jumped over the last obstacle—a high-jump hurdle—I thought I was going to pass out, but I made it. To this day, I might be the biggest, heaviest person to get over that wall and finish the obstacle course at the *Superstars* competition.

DANNY SNYDER

I will feel forever grateful and blessed for having played football for the Washington Redskins for ten seasons. Because of that, I would love to say that I have every confidence the Redskins are on the cusp of greatness, poised to return to the glory years.

However, honesty and good sense preclude me from making such predictions.

It's amazing how far the Redskins have plummeted since the Cooke family sold the franchise to Danny Snyder in 1999. "Danny's" Redskins have been to the playoffs only once since he took over—that was in Snyder's first year of ownership.

Not counting the expansion Houston Texans, the Redskins are one of only six teams who have failed to make the playoffs from 2000 through the 2004 seasons. Three of those teams—Cincinnati, Jackson, and Buffalo—were in the hunt in 2004 and have a much brighter future than the Washington Redskins.

Not counting interim coach Terry Robiskie, the Redskins have had four head coaches during Snyder's reign of terror—Norv Turner, Marty Schottenheimer, Steve Spurrier, and Joe Gibbs.

Where is the continuity? Where is the stability?

Spurrier may have never approached the same level of success he enjoyed at the college level, but he had to deal with a meddlesome Snyder.

"It started the second season when we were putting the team together, and our owner [Daniel Snyder] picked the QB," Spurrier said recently. "That's when I knew the thing wasn't going to work. As a coaching staff, we didn't pick the team."

Danny did the same thing when he forced Norv Turner to play Jeff George over Brad Johnson. In practice, Jeff George might be the best-looking quarterback in NFL history—in practice. In the games, Jeff George has never been a consistent winner.

Snyder made wholesale changes almost immediately. He fired more than two-dozen front office employees, including secretaries and most of the public relations staff. Now, I'm one of the first ones to say a good PR staff is an essential element to any NFL team—and good secretaries are worth every penny they are paid. But you don't turn around a football team with secretaries and public relations personnel. Secretaries don't block. PR types don't tackle.

John Konoza, a long-time member of the Redskins public relations department, returned to the team as public relations director shortly after Snyder took over. John recognized a no-win situation. After only three days—THREE DAYS—John resigned from the Redskins and went back to the automobile business.

Not that Danny doesn't recognize the need for public relations. I'm sure he pays big money to Michael Sitrick as his primary spokesman. Sitrick heads up Sitrick & Company, a Los Angeles-based public relations firm with offices in Washington. Sitrick & Company, known particularly for its crisis management, is described by the *Los Angeles Times* as "The Wizard of Spin." Sitrick's clients have included Orange County, California during its bankruptcy troubles in the mid-1990s, comedian Paula Poundstone after her child endangerment case, and the Los Angeles archdiocese following its sex scandals.

According to *Investor's Business Daily*, Sitrick's company specializes in "the contentious and controversial." That definitely constitutes a good fit with Danny Snyder, who seems more concerned with damage control than exercising good prior judgment or common sense.

You also can't improve the franchise simply by throwing money at it. Danny has treated the Washington Redskins as if the team were a Fantasy League football squad. He paid big money for big names who could contribute very little at the advanced stages of their careers—players like Bruce Smith, Deion Sanders, and Mark Brunell.

Snyder's moves have put the Redskins behind the eight ball as far as the salary cap goes. You have to have the right people to make the proper personnel decisions. You have to trust those people. Very early on, Snyder fired or forced out general manager Charlie Casserly, a valuable man in the organization for more than 20 years. The Redskins have yet to return to the playoffs since Charlie's departure.

For the most part, the Redskins' draft picks have been abysmal under Snyder. *Washington Post* columnist Sally Jenkins aptly described the Redskins' player development as "systemic rot" during Snyder's ownership.

◆   ◆   ◆

One of Danny's biggest schemes was to lure Joe Gibbs out of retirement for $25 million dollars. I almost feel like Jay Leno addressing Hugh Grant: "Joe, what in hell were you thinking?"

Even Joe's wife, Pat, told him, "You're going to ruin your good name." She probably made the comment in jest, but it's not that far off the mark. Joe Gibbs can still coach in the NFL, but he doesn't have the same people around him—no Bobby Beathard, no Charlie Casserly.

When Joe Gibbs decided he was coming back, he acted like Belushi and Akroyd recruiting their old band members in the *Blues Brothers*: "Hey, Breaux! Hey, Bugel! We're getting the band back together."

I truly believe Joe Gibbs loves the Washington Redskins; that was his primary motivation for his return to Washington. If Joe simply wanted to return to football, he had a tremendous opportunity with Arthur Blank in Atlanta. Blank owns Home Depot, the major sponsor for Gibbs's racing team. Gibbs was on the board of directors with the Falcons, and the team was firing Dan Reeves. In Arthur Blank, Gibbs would have worked for a hands-off owner. Instead, he labors under Danny Snyder— "Napoleon with a Cell Phone."

◆   ◆   ◆

Danny Snyder's arrogance and pomposity have quickly become legend around the NFL. As *New York Times* columnist Mike Freeman wrote, "It took the Oakland owner, Al Davis, a lifetime to irk the NFL, and the Dallas owner Jerry Jones a matter of years. But it has taken Snyder just a few months."

When Danny attended a Ravens-Redskins game in Baltimore, he decided the food in the owner's box was not up to his standards. He complained about it to Ravens owner Art Modell. Art blew him off, saying, "That's the food we've had since we've had the team here. It's been good enough for everyone else."

When the Ravens came to play the Redskins at FedEx Field, they drove down in seven team buses. The Redskins security only allowed three of the buses to drop off the players and personnel. The drivers of the other four buses with the rest of the team and Ravens owner Art Modell had to pay—$40 each—and were forced to park in the back lots. The Redskins did offer to reimburse the Ravens the $160 on Monday. Danny probably would have demanded interest.

On his first trip to Detroit, Danny was ticked off because his booth was obstructed—the television cameras couldn't get a shot of him in the booth. He wanted the Lions to do something about it right away. The next time he saw Lions president Matt Millen at the owner's meeting, he complained to him.

"Well, Danny, that's what we have," Matt told him. "We're not going to change it for you or anyone else."

Snyder quickly corrected him, "It's not Danny. It's Mr. Snyder."

"Well, Danny, that's just the way it is," Matt responded as he walked away.

On the Redskins' next trip to Detroit, when Snyder's advance team got to the owner's box in new Ford Field, they found the booth had not been cleaned from the week before. You know that came from upstairs. His advance team had to clean up the booth before he got there … popcorn and trash all over. That's how well-respected Snyder is in the NFL.

At Arizona, he got all honked off because the server in his booth was wearing an Arizona Cardinals tie. Imagine that: A team employee wearing a Cardinals tie. … How inconsiderate!

◆ ◆ ◆

Danny Snyder can't do anything unless he has his entourage with him. The biggest thrill for this pusillanimous man is to walk onto the field with 30 people behind him—including a couple bodyguards. Just like many of the new-age pro athletes, he needs his little posse wherever he goes to self-validate his importance.

His boorish behavior has become a model for some of his employees. Prior to a game with the Ravens—the same game where the Redskins charged the Ravens team bus to park—the Washington public address announcer berated the Ravens' fans, including the remark, "Ravens fans suck."

The childish behavior continued during the game. The Redskins band played loud music after the Ravens broke the huddle, and even continued when the Baltimore quarterback started to call the signals. That was a clear violation of an NFL anti-noise rule.

And it wasn't the first time Snyder's Redskins ignored the league mandate. Only three weeks earlier, they had pulled those stunts against Tampa Bay, resulting in a $20,000 fine. So then they went and pulled the same crap three weeks later. How smart is that?

◆ ◆ ◆

Danny paid a record $800 million to acquire the team in 1999. Since then, he has done everything possible to squeeze every last Redskin cent out of the fans. Teams usually raise ticket prices following a championship season or a move to a new stadium. Neither situation applies to Snyder, but he still increased the average ticket price by nearly 30 percent. The Redskins' average ticket price is the second highest in the National Football League. A ticket to a New England Patriots game may be a little pricier on average, but with three Super

Bowl championships in four years, the Patriots' price tag is a much greater value.

Snyder has also burdened the Redskins' fans with hefty increases in parking and concessions. The cost of game programs has more than tripled. Sandwiches can run as high as eight dollars.

Every year it's a different scam. One year the Redskins will say, "We're not raising ticket prices," so they raise the parking or concessions. The next year they don't raise parking or concessions, but they up the ticket prices. A typical family of four can't afford it, but they can drive 45 minutes up to the road to Baltimore and watch a better product in a better stadium with a better atmosphere for much less money.

In his second year of ownership, Snyder decided to charge fans ten dollars to watch a preseason practice. At the news conference to announce that decision, Steve Baldacci, the team president at the time, told the media many NFL teams did the same thing. It didn't take long for the media to jump on that lie. A handful of teams charged fans for parking. A few charged for special scrimmages against opposing teams. However, the Redskins were the first and only team that charged for everyday practice sessions. If you're going to gouge the fans, at least have the courage or decency to tell the truth about it.

In addition to serving as a shining example of Snyder's greed and a public relations fiasco, the decision to charge fans to watch practice sessions was incredibly stupid from an operational standpoint. Before they charged the fans, the Redskins could bar opposing scouts from attending the practices. Once they started to charge admission, it was fair game for everyone. A scout or representative from any team in the NFL could attend any practice; take pictures, and even videotape. They could watch and record every play and every formation in the Redskins' playbook.

The hits just kept coming. Early in 2005, the Redskins informed season ticket holders that if they wished to purchase their seats with a credit card, they would have to do it with the Redskins Extra Points MasterCard. I can understand encouraging the use of its brand card, but the Redskins wanted to force their fans to use only that card. The new credit-card restriction not only caused a huge public outcry but also caught the attention of MasterCard, which "requested" that the Redskins review their decision. Only a week after its installment, the Redskins dropped the new credit policy and continued to allow season ticket holders to use all brands of MasterCard. After reversing themselves, Danny's boys acted surprised that their restrictive policy wasn't received well.

In six years, Danny has cut out the hearts and trimmed the wallets of the Washington Redskins's fans. Danny Snyder has taken the Washington Redskins franchise and systematically removed the history and class from the organization brick by brick.